MORT!

NO PLACE

MORT!

TO HIDE

MORT!

BY *MORTON DOWNEY, JR.*
WITH WILLIAM HOFFER

DELACORTE PRESS / NEW YORK

ACKNOWLEDGMENT

This book simply could not have been written without the active assistance of Kim Downey and Marilyn Hoffer. Their input, in both content and style, was invaluable. Their ability to debate the issues helped to clarify many points. Their emotional support was immeasurable.

The fact that they are both beautiful blondes was merely a bonus.

Published by
Delacorte Press
The Bantam Doubleday Dell Publishing Group, Inc.
666 Fifth Avenue
New York, New York 10103

Library of Congress Cataloging in Publication Data

Downey, Morton.
Mort! Mort! Mort! : no place to hide / by Morton Downey, Jr. with William Hoffer.
p. cm.
ISBN 0-440-50092-3
1. United States—Social conditions—1980– 2. Social problems.
I. Hoffer, William. II. Title.
HN65.D69 1988
306'.0973—dc19 88-15007
CIP

Manufactured in the United States of America

September 1988

10 9 8 7 6 5 4 3 2 1

BG

Table
of
Contents

April 20, 1988

I went to my mailbox at my apartment this morning and pulled out my mail. On top was a letter post-marked Ontario, Canada, and it was addressed to Morton Downey, United States of America. It was then I knew for sure, there is no place to hide.

Morton Downey, Jr.

1
Loudmouth

$\triangleright$

For THIRTY YEARS A MOUTHFUL OF WHITE teeth has been my trademark. Back in the 1950s when I was a rock 'n' roll songwriter and singer, people remembered me for my blazing, buck-toothed white grin. Later, as a disc jockey in Cincinnati and Miami I became known as "Mighty Mouth" and "The Largest Mouth in the South." Through the years of my participation in civil rights demonstrations, my countenance sometimes angered white supremacists, for I appeared insolent, even though I did not try to do so.

In 1961, while driving north to assume a new job as a disc jockey at WICE in Boston, my foot slipped off the brake pedal and my car slammed into the tail-finned rear of a 1959 Chrysler Le Baron. I flew through the windshield of my car and landed on the trunk of the Chrysler, swallowing, not only my cigar, but seven of my front teeth.

It was a Boston dentist who capped my teeth, creating the wide, shiny grin that now blazes forth on the television screen.

There came a period of my life when I kept my pearly whites under wraps. I became a successful businessman, a Washington, D.C., lobbyist, and a sports entrepreneur, using the grin to ingratiate myself when necessary, but toning down, somewhat, my natural inclination to open my distinctive jaw and shoot off my loud mouth.

These were strange, searching years for me. Somewhere in my head was an unexplainable dissonance. The liberal fervor that colored my earlier years had waned, but I was not quite sure how to replace it. My heart still ached for the oppressed, the poor, the hungry, the sick, the wretches of the world who lived their lives in daily agony. I still believed fiercely in the stated goals of the liberal philosophy, but I looked around at the results and I could not escape the conclusion that *we had screwed it up!!!*

What went wrong?

I did not know, so I lived my life as best I could, maintained what was then a good, comfortable marriage, and raised my three daughters, preparing them for what I hoped would be a better world than I had experienced.

I found a relatively quiet outlet for my social goals by helping to finance and construct self-sufficient hospitals in Biafra, and this, finally, began to provide insights into my emerging sociopolitical orientation. Still, I kept relatively quiet.

Two things happened that convinced me to reopen my loud mouth. The first was one of the most despicable chapters in our national history: overnight, abortion became the most popular form of contraception. But, to me, abortion was murder, pure and simple. The second was the most beautiful event of my life: I met Kim.

The increasingly successful attempts to legalize abortion compelled me to speak. In the early 1970s I became one of the most vocal and most recognized defenders of the right of the unborn child to life, liberty, and the pursuit of happiness. Back then I was a single-issue advocate. I screamed bloody murder over abortion.

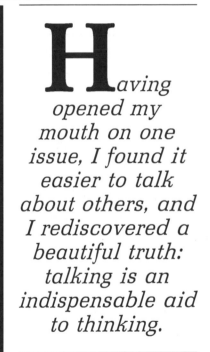

Having opened my mouth on one issue, I found it easier to talk about others, and I rediscovered a beautiful truth: talking is an indispensable aid to thinking.

Having opened my mouth on one issue, I found it easier to talk about others, and I rediscovered a beautiful truth: talking is an indispensable aid to thinking. The more I spoke out, the more my philosophies crystallized.

I realized very quickly that there was a nation of individuals out there who shared many of my convictions. Americans want to take care of Americans. There should be no hungry, no homeless, no jobless millions out there. Our young men and women should be trained for lives of meaningful contribution, lives that will enrich them and their fellow Americans. Our great masses of men and women should be working hard and loving it. Our aging population should be venerated for its wisdom; the rest of us should be sitting at their feet and listening. Our society should be harmonious, with equal opportunity for all—with no qualifications whatsoever.

These were my dreams, and the more I spoke of them, the more I realized they were shared by the vast majority of good men and women in our land.

They also shared with me, however, the same dismal conclusion. *We had screwed it up!!!* Or, which is only slightly less incriminating, we had allowed the politicians to do so.

Two hundred years had passed since patriots of incredible wisdom and almost superhuman guts had launched the American experiment. The new nation would be a democracy, where the people would rule. In practice, this is impossible, for we cannot put every minuscule issue up for a popular vote. So we settled for representative government. The people would elect a few to represent the many.

Now it was clear to me that this relatively simple and beautiful system had been perverted. I listened to the people and I listened to the politicians and I heard such a cacophony that I wanted to scream in agony. The politicians did not represent the people. They represented the interests of business or labor leaders or banks or doctors. In particular they represented the interests of lawyers. But they most assuredly did not represent the interests of the common folk. When they spoke, they said what the media wanted to hear, not what was in their hearts.

How did this come to be? Was it a manifestation of the phenomenon so widely proclaimed during the Bicentennial era? A nation can only remain great for two hundred years, they said. That's the maximum. Look at history.

Could it be?

The Romans lulled their people to sleep with hedonistic diversions, such as orgies, circuses, and the sight of bloody gladiators killing each other in the arena. Are we doing the same? We come home from work too exhausted to do anything but lie on the sofa. We turn on the television and what do we see? Orgies, circuses, and bloody gladiators killing each other. We are lulled to sleep just as Roman society was. As a result, our so-called leaders do as they please, just as the Roman dictators did.

We have, as a society, attempted to take the easy way out. We condone evil, instead of condemning it. We excuse it, psychoanalyze it, throw money at it, and medicate it, then turn our backs on it and hope it will go away.

This is what I saw with my own eyes, and this is what I heard others saying, too . . . others who, like me, feared that our great land of liberty was going down the tubes.

Then came Kim.

I was married twice before, although the first one really doesn't count. That was no more than a youthful fling, a rebellion against my father. It resulted in the miracle of my first-born daughter, Melissa, but little else. It ended almost overnight.

My second marriage was good for a decade, but soured in tandem with my career. An ill-advised business loan went bad, forcing me into bankruptcy. At about the same time Joan decided that she wanted, and deserved, a chance to be on her own. I agreed. The divorce was amicable; together we decided that I would continue to raise our two daughters, Tracey and Kelli. (Fatherly custody, gang, may be the only similarity between Phil Donahue and myself.)

So there I was with three daughters in tow, an economic life that was in disarray, and a message bursting inside me. I decided to return to my old vocation, one that would allow me to bare my soul to my countrymen and at the same time, perhaps, feed my children. I had always been able to communicate my deepest feelings through music. Now I determined to rebuild a singing career, this time in the country-and-western field.

I put a band together and we hit the road to gain some experience prior to a scheduled opening in Las Vegas. One night in 1977 I stood on the stage of a honky-tonk in Salina, Kansas, and as I sang my eyes kept returning to a beautiful young blonde in the audience. During my break I went over to meet her. She resisted me at first, but not for long.

Three months later we were married.

Kim is an imaginative, assertive person. By the calendar she is many years younger than I, but in experience she is my peer. She is the other half of my soul.

I found myself mated to a woman who, albeit in her own style, has a loud mouth of her own. She will argue out any issue with me, and as often as not, alter my opinion by the force of pure logic. We are teacher and student to one another. We are best friends.

It was Kim who persuaded me that I had a duty to air my views to the world, and here is how we decided to do it. We were living in Orlando. One day in 1982 Kim saw an advertisement. A radio station was looking for a talk show host. "You can do it," she said. "You *should* do it."

I answered the ad, but only after Kim and I had come to an agreement. She desired a career of her own, and I want her to have that. But ours is not a two-career marriage. It takes the strength of two to support and nurture one career. So here was the deal: because

I was older, I would take the first shot. I would have ten years; then it would be Kim's turn.

Five years and four radio stations later, I host the most widely viewed prime-time television talk show in America. Tens of millions of people listen to my loud mouth every night. Kim was right; I did have something to say, and people wanted to hear it.

The average age of my audience is thirty-two, which makes them the cream of yuppiedom. Yet they become engrossed in topics that are almost exclusively political. On my show they do not get the sociosexual pap that Phil, Oprah, Geraldo, Sally Jessy, and so many others give them. Why do they choose to listen to a fifty-five-year-old former liberal activist, an ex-con who's been married three times, a man who would self-describe his major accomplishments as the creation of songs and poetry?

The answer must be that they like what they hear, and this is not an idle statement. Music and its poetry are part and parcel of my message because *there is no better means of tapping our innermost thoughts.* Let me explain.

I was twelve years old when I wrote my first song, inspired or, rather, upset by my mother and father's divorce. I called the song "Money, Marbles, and Chalk":

> *My love has left, flown away*
> *Ain't got nobody no more.*
> *Like a bird sprouting wings,*
> *She's flown out to sea,*
> *And I am alone on the shore.*

> *I've got money, marbles, and chalk, sweetheart,*
> *But I still feel like I'm poor.*

> *'Cause my money won't spend,*
> *And my marbles won't roll,*
> *And my chalk won't write any more.*

My father took one look at those lyrics and sent me off on my one and only visit to a psychiatrist. But I did not need a shrink; what my father did not understand (nor did I at the time) was that writing the song was my therapy.

The style of popular music varies from age to age, but the essence never changes. It is the poetic voice by which the masses communicate. Music is a very special window to the soul, and if we learn to peer through it, we gain insights into the current state of society. This is because music has a special derivation. Physiologists can trace the origin of brain waves, and know with certainty that speech comes from the left side of the brain, while music comes from the right. This explains why country-and-western singer Mel Tillis stutters heavily when he speaks, but sings in smooth, golden tones.

There is knowledge here upon which we should capitalize. We all believe it is beneficial to talk out our problems, but we ignore the fact that it is also possible to sing them out. When we speak, only half of our brain is revealed to the world. The other half, containing a deeper, more hidden persona, struggles to be heard also, but it does not possess the ability to speak. Music is perhaps its major outlet.

Thus, when we create or enjoy music, we are able to make contact with the other half of humanity, and we often hear surprising messages.

Consider the music of the past thirty years. The explosion of rock 'n' roll in the mid-1950s, personified by Elvis Presley, was prophetic. We could not yet put it

into words, but the music made us *feel* that we stood upon the threshold of change, whether for good or ill. Bob Dylan, in the early sixties, set the mood for protest. The Beatles' music switched from lighthearted twaddle to introspective, shapeless paeans to spirituality; its very sound fabricated a druglike high in the right brain of the listener. Was there ever a more stirring call for humans to love and help one another than Simon and Garfunkel's "Bridge Over Troubled Water"? Listening to that, how could we not help but want to become socially involved?

Times changed, and so did the music. To this observer's ear, the music of the past decade has grown more violent and angry. Twisted Sister's "We're Not Gonna Take It" and Michael Jackson's "Bad" are telling us something. And we should listen. They are telling us: *We have screwed it up.*

Whether or not we appreciate pop music, we should study its content carefully, for it is telling us what messages are flashing out from the right sides of people's brains—messages that they cannot communicate in any other way. Rock 'n' roll, along with country-and-western music, are the means by which otherwise ordinary men and women send their deepest messages to one another, and these messages are far more relevant than any pompous, unintelligible rhetoric spouted by pseudointellectuals such as William F. Buckley, Jr., who would have difficulty communicating with a horse's ass if he did not identify so well with it.

Those who would ban popular music, or put constraints upon it in any way, choose to ignore very important societal messages.

I do not appreciate songs that talk about screwing or snorting or mainlining, but I do appreciate the fact that they are free expressions from people who are trying to tell us something—not just the performer, but the listener also. If a song with aberrant lyrics gains a popular following, it is because those lyrics have found a point of commonality between singer and audience.

I do not buy the contention that listening to such music makes one go out and rape and kill and procure drugs. If it only takes three minutes of music to motivate you to rape and kill and contaminate your bloodstream, then you were probably unfit for society in the first place. John Wayne Gacy was a great aficionado of classical music, and a sexual aberrant who murdered thirty-four men and boys in Chicago. Are we therefore to ban Beethoven and Mozart?

Of course not.

When the audience files into the television studio prior to my show, it hears loud contemporary rock 'n' roll music. This is not an idle distraction, but a purposeful action. It pumps up the audience and it pumps up me.

We tape at 7:15 P.M., at the end of a long, busy day of preparation. At the very time when others are at home relaxing, I must reach my mental and emotional peak. Loud rock 'n' roll music helps me accomplish this.

The next hour will bring a torrent of words from my guests, my audience, and my own loud mouth. I want those words, as much as possible, to illuminate the entire personality of the speaker, exhibiting not only the logic supplied by the left side of the brain, but the feelings buried in the right side. Music is a pipeline that can free those emotions. The throbbing beat of rock 'n' roll—the music of the masses—evokes the heartbeat of the masses. It focuses us all on the expectation that something *alive* is going to happen shortly: people are going to communicate.

And that is sweet music, indeed.

It helps us to accomplish something that is rare on television.

We *Have Given the Common Man and Woman a Forum.*

We have given the common man and woman a forum.

The media in general are guilty of a shortsighted, patronizing attitude. You can read it and hear it clearly in their words. *They do not respect the opinions of the average American. They do not believe that you have the ability to reason through the important issues of our time and reach rational conclusions.*

This is, of course, the same kind of crap upon which politicians feed. Our political leaders operate upon the assumption that they—not you—know what is best for America.

Even the most widely viewed talk-show hosts exhibit the same philosophy. Phil Donahue runs a promotional spot for his show, recalling how in the early days he discovered the wisdom of taking a microphone into the audience and eliciting comments. But listen closely to Donahue and his reaction to the comments. If someone in the audience happens to agree with the host's own liberal, bleeding-heart stance on the given issue, Donahue will praise the person for his or her insight. But if the comment runs counter to Donahue's views, he will denigrate it, albeit politely, and imply that the speaker is unenlightened and misguided. Furthermore, Donahue has a tendency to load his audience with people concerned over the given issue, rather than with representatives from the normal world.

Donahue, to me, is the epitome of what I call the liberal pabulum-puker. His solution to any problem is simplistic and based upon psychoanalytical baby food. In Donahue's view of the world, an individual is rarely responsible for his or her own

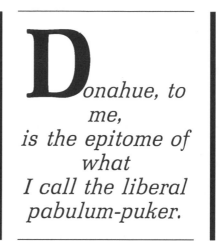

Donahue, to me, *is the epitome of what I call the liberal pabulum-puker.*

actions; rather, society is at fault. There is no good and evil in the world; everything is liberally shaded with gray.

I applaud Donahue for his effort to get people to speak. If only he would listen . . .

Our show, on the other hand, was built upon the philosophy that everyone not only has something to say and has a right to say it, but that we have a duty to truly listen to and respect the opinion of anyone. I may be the host—someone has to be—but that does not make me right. It does not make my opinion more valid than yours. Everyone has a compelling story to tell, but rarely do they find a forum where people will listen.

We decided to give people that forum at either one of our two Loudmouth podiums set up in the studio. And from the beginning, we realized that we had tapped a raw American nerve. Like Peter Finch in the movie *Network,* average Americans stood up at our Loudmouths and proclaimed, "We're mad as hell and we're not going to take it anymore!" The Loudmouth was a soapbox in Hyde Park. Anyone could stand up there and confront the so-called experts. The common man and woman suddenly had available a form of free speech never before allowed on television.

Critics have labeled my audience intolerable, obnoxious, and abusive.

To them I say: *Watch the show!* and *Listen carefully!* You will hear something you never heard on television before. You will hear the voice of the people. You will hear people who are very fair, but who realize it is no longer fair to remain quietly on the sidelines as politicians and pabulum-pukers let this great nation go to hell.

You will hear people demanding change—demanding it of themselves and of their leaders.

You will hear people ready and able to hiss and boo and throw ridicule at pompous authority, but—and this is key—*only after each individual has a chance to voice his or her own opinion.*

Here I will make a great admission: I am not perfect. Sometimes—frequently—someone on my show will make a comment so counter to my philosophies that I will cut him off in mid-sentence. I get mad. I get very mad. The right side of my brain cries for expression and my loud mouth screams in frustration. But when I realize that this has occurred, I make every attempt to give the person a chance to air his full viewpoint.

Am I fair? Probably not, which makes me as fair as anyone else. It is generally the liberal who angers me the most, probably because I am so tired of hearing him get far more than equal time on the media.

But I hope that my capped teeth are the only phony part of the show. Consider the testimony of Tony Pedesta, founder of People for the American Way. I like Tony very much, even though I abhor his politics.

He is the archetype of the pabulum-puking liberal. He has been silenced by my audience chanting *To-nee! To-nee! To-nee!* which brought from him the comment, "The definition of a fool is someone who appears on this show twice." But Tony said that during his *second* appearance on the show, and he added, "Have me on again." I applaud his willingness to air his views to an obviously hostile host and audience—but I still abhor his politics.

Verbal ridicule has a historic heritage in this country. What better way is there to let a speaker know that you believe he is full of empty words?

If this loudmouth approach has done nothing else, it has drawn the audience out of its lethargy. The common man and woman have risen. And we must listen.

I do not claim to be the exclusive voice of the people, but my experience on television has led me to believe that many of my opinions are shared by a great multitude. They are strong opinions. What good are half-hearted ideas when we are talking about happiness and misery, life and death, good and evil? I do not have any more right to express these opinions than you do . . . which is to say, I have every right in the world to express them.

And more. I have a duty to express them.

I have spent a lifetime formulating the opinions detailed in the following pages. They may or may not be right, but I sure as hell think they are. You may or may not agree with them. You may love or hate the solutions I propose. Some of them would be relatively easy to implement, some would be difficult. Some might fail, but they would fall to the ground with no heavier a *thud* than the socialistic "solutions" attempted during the past three decades.

Read them.

Think about them.

Then find your own forum to air your own opinions. Become a loudmouth yourself.

It would be easier for me to keep silent. What follows is going to bring a tidal wave of criticism down upon me. It will anger lawyers, news reporters, doctors, psychiatrists, feminists, abortionists, teachers, criminologists, the leaders of certain South American nations, labor union officials, sexual perverts, and all the bureaucratic administrators of what I call America's poverty industry. Most of all it will anger the politicians who are traitors to the expressed will and latent potential of the American people.

Yes, gang, what follows will make me more unpopular than ever with the people who continue to run this country in their own way, forcing you to accept their "solutions" because they believe they are smarter than you. But I cannot keep silent anymore. The stakes are too high. I saw the British Empire topple in forty years. I believe our own society will crumble, too, within the next twenty years . . . unless we do something about it.

I *cannot keep silent. There is no place to hide.*

I cannot keep silent. There is no place to hide.

Some will call me a racist; read carefully and you will see that I am not.

No one will call me a liberal, yet some of my proposed solutions are decidedly so.

Pabulum-puking liberals will call me an extreme

conservative, a "storm trooper of the right"; read carefully, and you will see that I am not.

What I am is what I believe most Americans to be: neither Democrat nor Republican, neither liberal nor conservative, but someone willing to listen to all philosophies and fine-tune them to my own beliefs, someone searching for solutions that will work for all Americans, not just the segmented few.

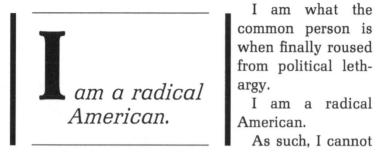

I am a radical American.

I am what the common person is when finally roused from political lethargy.

I am a radical American.

As such, I cannot shut my loud mouth. So fasten your seat belts, gang, we are about to do what we do on television every night:

Kick ass!!!

2
Politicians

ALL MY LIFE I'VE KNOWN POLITICIANS ON A personal level. I grew up with the Kennedys. I worked with the Reverend Jesse Jackson in the Civil Rights Era. I worked in the campaigns of Jack and Bobby Kennedy, Pierre Salinger, and Senator Fritz Hollings of South Carolina. I am personally well acquainted with Teddy Kennedy, Gary Hart, George McGovern, Richard Nixon, Phil Crane, Henry Hyde, Al Gore, and many others. I have had, therefore, a unique opportunity to observe that politicians are real people with the same emotions and weaknesses as everyone else.

It would amaze me if politicians did not succumb to their failings, just like the rest of us. Of course many of them sleep around. Of course many of them succumb to greed. Of course many of them lie, steal, and cheat on their income taxes. In this telecommunications age, they appear to us larger than life, but, of course, they are not.

Let's think about this. We are a great experiment in democracy, the world's last best hope. We are, in theory, a people who rule ourselves. In one of the most critical decisions ever made concerning the future of our experiment, George Washington refused the trappings of royalty to emphasize that this was to be a government wherein otherwise ordinary people assumed temporary roles to see to the management of the country. There were those who continually attempted to elevate Washington to a quasi-royal status, and he consistently refused.

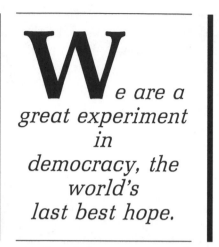

W*e are a* great experiment *in* democracy, the *world's* last best hope.

Over the course of two hundred years we have lost sight of the role of the politician. Through the impact of the media, slick advertisers, and cagy press agents, we have allowed politicians to assume an air of royalty. They have responded by becoming a royal pain in the ass.

In some ways this is our fault more so than theirs. We treat them as something greater than ordinary people, and few humans can resist the lure of royal treatment. It does not take a politician long to begin to believe that he is special.

The original democratic concept was that a politician was to serve the people, but today's average American politician believes it is better to receive than give. There are givers and takers throughout this world, and politicians fall into the latter category. When they run for office, they take up your time, asking you to help them campaign. They take your money and use it to buy votes. They take your most precious American possession, your very own vote. Once they are in office, they take your tax dollars and build programs that tend to benefit their particular circle of friends. They raise your taxes so that they can keep giving themselves pay raises.

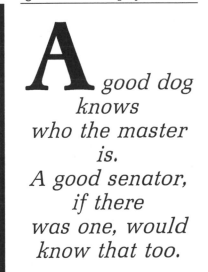

A *good dog knows who the master is. A good senator, if there was one, would know that too.*

The most useful and compassionate Senator I know should be a model for all politicians. Loyalty and love are his strong points. Should an enemy darken my doorstep he would personally defend me, for my welfare is more important to him than his very own. He would stand by my side to the death, if necessary, but at times when I wish to be free to live my own life without interference, he will obey me and leave. Yet the moment I return, he will welcome me with unrestrained enthusiasm. For all of his devotion, he asks little in return beyond the basic creature comforts; if need be, he would subsist upon dog food alone, and not complain.

Senator is my nine-year-old Doberman pinscher. Compared to him, all the other senators are true sons of bitches.

This is not too farfetched an analogy. A good dog knows who the master is. A good senator, if there was one, would know that too.

But, alas, most of them are like "Senator Paperman," the subject of a song I composed many years ago.

Senator Paperman

Paper your walls with your bills,
Sick legislation designed to cure all of our ills.
Your special interests
Are
Gas, oil, and booze.
Lobbyists feed you,
So
How can you lose?
Down with you, Paperman,
Damn,
You're a paper-thin man.

I have known only a few politicians who really seemed to believe their civics primer, and the most memorable was Tommy McGrath, who represented the Atlantic City area of New Jersey in the mid-sixties. The chances are excellent that you never heard of him. During his single term in Congress, Tommy did not introduce any pork barrel legislation. He did not support any legislation that would throw dollars into the pockets of construction contractors in his district, or do anything to strengthen his local Teamsters' Union, or benefit any other special-interest group in his district. He suffered from a critical liability as a modern politician, in that he was quiet, shy, and nondemonstrative. He was not the type to shout out his message and awaken people from their collective siesta; he was simply naive enough to try to help everyone in his district. As a result, he built no major sources of campaign contributions and, of course, was beaten soundly when he ran for reelection.

This did not stop Tommy from his life's mission of helping other people. For the next several years he worked with Father Tom Rooney and me to build self-sufficient hospitals in Biafra.

We need more Tommy McGraths in elected office today. He is the type of true politician whom people want in office but do not know how to elect. The common American knows that he is not getting representative government and craves it,

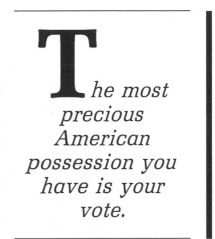

The most precious American possession you have is your vote.

but the never-changing election results and the self-serving actions of the reigning politicos have beaten us down to the point where we see only futility. We have come to the same cynical conclusion as George Orwell in *1984,* when he asserted that political rhetoric is designed to achieve three purposes: make lies appear as truth; make murder a merciful act; and give solidarity to a breeze.

I repeat: The most precious American possession you have is your vote, but look what Americans are doing with that great privilege. In 1960, 62.8 percent of the eligible voters in the nation cast ballots for President. Over the next quarter century that percentage declined steadily. By 1984, only 53.3 percent of the eli-

gible voters bothered to make their presidential choice known. Why do 46 percent of us squander our most precious possession?

The answer, of course, is that we believe our vote is futile. We have resigned ourselves to the dismal fact that politicians may differ in style but are the same in substance. They are all takers.

If you sat on your duff on election day, frittering away your one chance in four years to have a say in who leads the country, chances are it was because you said to yourself:

- My vote won't count.
- None of the candidates has charisma.
- None of the candidates represents my thinking.
- Once they get into office, they won't listen to me anyway.

Look at those common concepts. Some people call them excuses not to vote, but they are not excuses, they are reasons. They have validity. People are fed up with their politicians, plain and simple. We have sent zillions of politicians to Washington, and what have they done for us?

Squat!

How do we change that?

First, put into place a long-proposed change in the presidential election process.

The framers of the Constitution knew that the average voter, two hundred years ago, had no real means of judging a presidential candidate. It was impossible to stump the country on horseback. They established the Electoral College so that local voters could make a knowledgeable choice from among a group of persons they did know. These electors were not to be tied to one particular candidate but were truly to represent their constituents. They would use their judgment to make a reasonable choice, as agents of the people.

Today you can get to anywhere in the world on twenty-four hours' notice . . . or express a letter in your stead. You can punch a few buttons on a cheap plastic machine, bounce electronic signals off of a satellite, and speak to almost anyone you care to reach—in milliseconds. You can send data the same way. You can sit at the keyboard of your personal computer, at work or at home, and learn all you'll ever care to know about the penguin population of Antarctica or the three busiest streets in Nairobi. And you can sit on your living-room floor in your underwear and follow every nuance of a presidential election campaign.

Why the hell do you need an electoral college?

You don't.

But the politicians do. It is one of their most effective weapons to promote political apathy, and here is how it works. Because of the winner-take-all system, whereby all of a state's electoral votes go to the candidate who wins that state, you must be in a majority in your state or your vote does not count.

Suppose you were one of the 53.3 percent of eligible Americans who voted in the 1984 presidential election.

If you live in Minnesota or the District of Columbia and you voted for the reelection of President Reagan, your vote did not count, because those two jurisdictions gave a majority vote to the Mondale-Ferraro ticket. On the other hand, if you voted for Mondale and lived anywhere else, your vote did not count, because all of the other states gave a majority to the President.

Thus it was that 1,061,612 Republican votes and a whopping 36,240,443 Democratic votes meant nothing. By 11 P.M. on election night, some 37 million Americans had to wonder why they bothered to vote.

It is no wonder that, every four years, the percentage of eligible voters drops.

This is no great new information. Everyone in politics knows that sooner or later the Electoral College is going to get us into trouble. We are going to elect one candidate on the basis of electoral votes even though the other candidate received a greater popular vote.

This continuing existence of the Electoral College is the second greatest example proving that politicians do not represent the average American (for the greatest example, see the chapter on taxes). The American people want to elect their President. They see no need —and plenty of potential for abuse—to send a bunch of political cronies off on a boondoggle to Washington so that they can run through the tired formality of "electing" a President who was truly elected weeks earlier.

It is long past time to scrap the Electoral College. A vote is a vote. Let the people decide.

And while we are at it, how about allowing the people to elect the person who holds the second-highest office? Who says the Vice President has to be a ventriloquist's dummy wired to mouth "Hail to the Chief"? Must we continue to choose the person who will stand a "heartbeat away from the Presidency" on the basis of geographically and ideologically balancing the ticket?

Why not have a little loyal opposition in the Vice President's office? Keep the old boy on his toes.

Next, let us remove from politicians their greatest public relations tool, the element that, more than any other, provides them with their royal aura. Let us ban *all* political advertising. Use the media to report on campaigns, to air debate, to cover the issues—and nothing more. As long as we allow politicians to pur-

chase advertising time and space, we will allow them
to purchase false images. Let's get back to deciding
elections upon the basis of issues, rather than who can
purchase the slickest advertising image.

We must find, and support, a new breed of politician.
Today's campaigner constantly walks on eggshells, trying not to offend anyone. This results in candidates
who are bland and spineless. To bring us out of our
political doldrums we need more politicians who are
willing to stake their chances of victory upon a single
issue.

Sure we need capable men and women to address
all the important issues, but life is complex. We also
need specialized politicians who will take a stand on
one issue at a time. Life is made up of single issues.

The American people are not in search of the perfect
candidate. We are realistic enough to know that such
an individual does not exist. But we are looking for a
candidate who truly has something to say—some
strong position with which we can identify. Is there not
one available politician who will tackle one major societal problem and deal with it until it is solved before
he moves on?

Reform is needed in another broad area. Who was it
who decided that the vast majority of politicians
should be lawyers? Where are the bank tellers and
bricklayers, the mechanics and meatcutters, the secretaries and salesmen? If we are ever going to get representative government, gang, we are not going to get it
by acting as if membership in the American Bar Association was a prerequisite to membership in Congress.
Let us vote in some men and women who know what it
means to get their hands dirty by some other means
than accepting dubious campaign contributions.

In the meantime, *do not give up hope*. Even in the

face of apathy and doubt we must exercise our right to vote. Vote first. Only then do you have the right to criticize the results.

We must continue to pursue the dream that if enough of the common people vote we *can* achieve common goals. We must not succumb to the polished media images that lure us to regard politicians with awe. We must remind them who works for whom.

We have allowed these nonrepresentative representatives to lull us into a feeling that government is something separate from us. We have forgotten that we *are* the government. We have lost the taste to govern ourselves. We must launch a great national movement to bring the country back to the people. America is ready for the citizen-politician to come to the forefront of the political scene. It is time to send real people to Washington. We can get rid of those bastards anytime we want to, from within the voting booth.

You bet it can happen.

But it better happen soon.

3
Lawyers

We may have more lawyers in this country than in the rest of the world combined. Everything we do is regulated by an intricate system of law, and here is the scary thing: Lawyers write the laws.

My father's greatest ambition for me was that I would become a lawyer, but for some reason that I could not identify at the time, the sight of a lawyer at work caused me a great deal of trepidation and inner combat.

I had numerous opportunities to see lawyers ply their trade, for, starting when I was about seven years old my parents became embroiled in an epic battle for custody of their five children. Since I was one of the five, one of the prizes in the legal war, I was intensely interested.

In the thirties and forties it was rare for a man to win custody of his children, yet my father was successful throughout some nine years of suits, countersuits, and appeals. Why? In theory, he won because the law rightly perceived him as the more competent parent. But in practice, he won because he could afford the more competent lawyers.

Was it any wonder that my father used to say, "Lawyers have a license to steal"?

If that was true, why did he want me to become a lawyer?

Both of my parents were prominent in show business. With her father, Richard, and her sisters, Joan and Constance, Barbara Bennett—my mother—had achieved fame as part of a dance team. All three sisters had gone on to movie careers. My father was a renowned tenor, having sung with Paul Whiteman's orchestra and later launched his own career in movie musicals. My father often told me how he met my mother. In his version of the story, he was starring in what was to be the first talking motion picture, *Syncopation* (although *The Jazz Singer* was released earlier); Mother had a bit part in the film. After they met and married, Barbara Bennett devoted her attention to hearth and home.

It was my mother's unfortunate lot to forsake all control of the purse strings. Thus, years later, when the marriage broke down, it was my father who possessed the wherewithal to hire the better lawyers. First, he used Ray Baldwin, a former governor of Connecticut. Later, when Baldwin was appointed to the bench, my father hired Adrian Mahr, a former attorney general for the state.

As a child, I could not comprehend the advantages of their political connections. Now, of course, I realize that they were respected members of the local old boys' network. They belonged to all the right clubs. They knew whom to play golf with. They knew which charities to support and which campaigns needed contributions. They even knew whom to kneel beside at church on Sunday mornings.

Their aura was nearly overwhelming, and it would have been easy to succumb to it. Yet, on the many occasions when I was forced to sit in a courtroom and participate in another round of the interminable custody battle, I could not escape the conclusion that these larger-than-life lawyers were little more than hired liars. Time after time I heard them portray my own mother as a drunk, a prostitute, and whatever else that was bad. It was extremely difficult for me to understand why they were allowed to say that, why they were allowed to tell these lies in open court, reducing my mother to tears.

It would be many years before I came to realize that courtroom success has little to do with truth or justice. Rather, the courtroom is a stage, whereupon the best actor wins. I have seen some of the

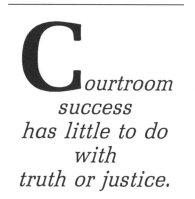

Courtroom success has little to do with truth or justice.

best of them at work—Marvin Mitchelson, Percy Foreman, Edward Bennett Williams, Racehorse Haynes—and they are all showmen. They are Shakespearean actors without wigs and makeup. And they play to their audience, the judge and jury, bringing to the bar the accumulated experience of their years of theatrical work. Sure, on some levels they must point out the effects of law upon the case, but they have hordes of assistants to handle those details. The job of the superstar lawyer has little or nothing to do with law. His job is to emotionalize the issue, causing the jury to respond emotionally. In many instances the final determination is made on the basis of emotion rather than law.

So be it. In an imperfect world we may have to accept the fact that juries will forever decide legal issues on the basis of an emotional bias. This, in fact, is not such an unworkable system if you happen to be a) rich, b) poor, or c) willing to sacrifice an important part of your body.

Let's look at the facts. Lawyers' fees rise in direct proportion to their reputations. The only way you can afford a superstar lawyer is to be rich, either individually or corporately. If you can afford an attorney who charges $250 an hour, and you can remain calm enough not to wince at every extra minute he spends on the job, then you have an excellent chance of winning your case.

On the other hand, if you are poor and cannot afford a lawyer, the court will appoint one for you. This is certainly not as good an alternative as the rich man's, but it has a sort of lottery aspect to it. In many areas of the country all lawyers have to accept a certain number of indigent cases; thus, the poor defendant stands a gambler's chance of obtaining at least a local superstar.

The common person generally has to pay an arm or a leg for a high-priced lawyer. Or perhaps an eye. The more gruesome the disfigurement, the more likely you are to persuade a competent lawyer to take your case on a percentage basis. The tremendous amounts paid out today in personal injury cases have nothing to do with the plight of the victims; rather, they are the direct result of the fact that the amount of the settlement is part and parcel of the lawyer's fee.

I am not one to defend doctors, but I do sympathize with their current legal plight. Doctors today are absolutely frightened to practice medicine. If anything goes wrong, they will be sued for zillions of dollars. Pick up the newspaper on any given day and you are likely to read reports of settlements in the $2- to $5-million range, or more.

Let's analyze this. Recently a jury awarded $7 million to a young man who had been crippled. That's a horrible fate, and my guess is that he would forsake every penny of the money if he could have the use of his legs back. The fact of the matter is that the loss is incalculable, but our legal system has made a determined effort to put a pricetag on it anyway. The defendant must pay the medical bills, of course. On top of that there must be compensation for the loss of earning power. Add to that total money for pain and suffering and loss of sexual compatibility with his partner (another form of pain and suffering).

In this case, the victim was a sixth-grade dropout. I do not begrudge this unfortunate individual adequate compensation, but how in the world did a jury arrive at a figure of $7 million for a sixth-grade dropout? Analyze his earning potential, throw in the cost of medical care, add a generous portion of pain, suffering, and sexual deprivation, and it still falls far short of $7 million.

The excessive amount of the settlement is due in large part to this: Every member of the jury, as well as the judge, is aware of the fact that the victim will never see the full $7 million. Who, sitting on a jury today, could not be aware that the lawyer is going to rake off one-third of the settlement? Want to give the plaintiff $5 million? Then you have to award $7 million so that

he will have some left after the lawyer takes his
bloated slice.

Ignoring the fact that the $5 million may be exces-
sive, why does society have to undergo another $2 mil-
lion worth of pain and suffering to pay for an ambu-
lance-chasing lawyer?

And it *is* society (you and me) who pays. Sure,
maybe the actual money comes from an insurance
company, but the insurance company raises its rates,
doctors raise their fees, and the common man and
woman get stuck with the tab. It all has a direct effect.

The legal system in this country does not benefit the
people in the middle of the spectrum. The rich, by definition, can afford anything they want. The poor have
public defenders and legal aid. It is the middle class
that cannot afford to pay for its constitutionally guaranteed protections.

It has always been my understanding that laws, in
theory, are made to protect the many and not just the
few, but that is not happening in practice. We seem
unable to make the legal system responsive to the
needs of the many. It is symptomatic of this attitude
that the common man cannot read or understand the
law. Why? Because lawyers write the laws, and they
have perceived the catch-22 in that incestuous relationship. If they write only convoluted laws full of legal
mumbo-jumbo, then the common man will have to hire
a lawyer to do things that our ancestors accomplished
with plain old common sense and, perhaps, a hand-
shake—things like buying or selling a house, firing a
nonproductive worker, or attempting to pass on to
one's children the meager results of a life of labor. In
fact, by the time you read this, you are probably not
getting the full impact of my thoughts, because a bat-
tery of lawyers have "toned down" the words. The *first*

thing my editor plans to do with this manuscript is to turn it over to lawyers.

We have allowed lawyers to create an environment wherein we are prisoners of fear, unable to settle our differences one on one. Should you be walking down the street with your wife and overhear a man make a nasty remark about her, you had better run to a phone and call your lawyer before you punch him in the nose.

Perhaps the worst part of this is that our courts are overwhelmed by the weight of cases that could and should be handled with simplicity, and, as a result, prevent us from concentrating upon important societal issues.

We have allowed the creation of a

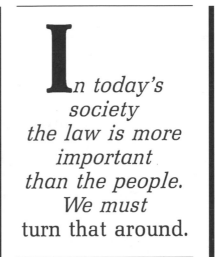

In today's society the law is more important than the people. We must turn that around.

system that produces more difficulties than it prevents, because we have allowed lawyers to convince us of a hidden truth that no lawyer would openly admit. In today's society, the law is more important than the people. We *must* turn that around.

The only way to change the current system of abuse is to provide something that the Constitution supposedly guarantees—equal access under the law —and that means equal whether you are rich, poor, or in between. It is time for this nation to adopt something similar to the system I first proposed in 1971, when I ran unsuccessfully for the Virginia state legislature. The

program would be called something like Judicare,
wherein everyone would pay a certain fee for compre-
hensive legal coverage, just as we now fund health insurance. In many cases it could be an employee benefit
(and already is in a few enlightened companies).
Whenever you needed a lawyer you would get a list of
those available. We currently have a glut of lawyers in
this country, and there would be countless numbers
willing to take Judicare cases. An important facet of
the program would be built-in incentives to settle the
case quietly, quickly, efficiently, and fairly, by taking it
—not to court—but to arbitration boards made up of
common citizens.

We would pay for Judicare through voluntary contributions, perhaps shared by employer and employee, as
we do with Social Security. It is critical that not one
penny would be contributed by the government, however, for when the government pays for anything it
slowly but surely extends its pernicious control. And
since lawyers control the government, they would soon
subvert the intent of Judicare. The simple fact is that
law is too important to be left in the hands of lawyers.

Even the superstars would have to donate a certain
amount of their time to Judicare, and why not? Almost
every lawyer who goes through school today benefits
from student loans, guaranteed by the government.
Let's get a benefit back for the American people. Let's
require lawyers to allocate a certain percentage of
their time to help those less fortunate than they—all of
the rest of us who do not happen to be lawyers.

Until that happens, lawyers leave us with only one
dismal alternative, and I came face to face with it in
1969 when I was sued for half a million dollars in a
case involving the American Basketball Association.
The details of that case are part of another subject,

addressed elsewhere in this book, but the noteworthy point here is that I did not have the money to hire a lawyer of any ilk. I was earning about $25,000 a year, which was pretty good in 1969, but already legal fees had gone beyond the realm of the common man. Yet I was far too successful to get any help from legal aid.

Since the case involved an important social issue championed by liberals, I approached the American Civil Liberties Union, seeking help. The American Basketball Association apparently sounded too rich for them, and they refused to take the case. I tried

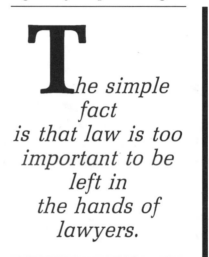

The simple fact is that law is too important to be left in the hands of lawyers.

numerous lawyers in New Orleans. The case was controversial and, in a sense, exciting. Unfortunately, I was on the wrong side of the controversy. No one would take the case on a *pro bono* basis; that is, for no fee, in order to champion an important but unpopular social cause. I was thus reduced to one of the most pitiable situations a man or woman can face in a modern American courtroom. I had to defend myself.

Put me one on one with another human being and I am ready and eager to argue my point, as is just about anyone. But put me—or any other ordinary citizen—into a courtroom populated and controlled by lawyers who lunch together and swap dirty stories in the hallways and whose existence is made necessary by the body of confusing law that they and their compatriots both wrote and are charged to enforce, and the result is intimidation. Your ears burn with the whispered chuckles of lawyers concocting variations of the aphorism that anyone who represents himself before the bar has a fool for a client.

The first thing I had to do was waive any right to appeal the fact that I didn't have a lawyer. It did not matter that the judge would not appoint a public defender in spite of the fact that I could not afford competent legal help. If I lost this case, I could not have the decision overturned because I was such a foolish client. The judge put the fear of God into me, then shook his head, and started the trial.

I was no Perry Mason. I wrested no courtroom confessions from my antagonists. I merely went about my business, presented my witnesses, and allowed the jury to determine whether they were truthful and believable. I was lucky to face a jury of my peers—normal, thoughtful, fair-minded American men and women (not a lawyer among them) who believed my witnesses, agreed with my points, and threw the plaintiff's case out of court.

I recommend this to no one, unless he or she is backed into a corner. But if the lawyers of this country fail you as they failed me, you can do worse than depend upon yourself. You can state your case, just like any other free human being, and trust that your peers on the jury are as attuned as yourself to the shortcomings of the American legal system.

Keep in mind this quotation from Shakespeare's *King Henry VI, Part II:*
    "The first thing we do,
    let's kill all the lawyers."

4

Euthanasia

In 1977 I received a letter from a man in Boston who wrote me in desperation because I had identified myself as an outspoken critic of euthanasia. I could almost feel the tears dripping from the page of his letter.

He was seventy-one and retired from his career, although he now worked nights as a security guard to help supplement his income. He needed the extra money, because he suffered from kidney disease and had to undergo dialysis treatments twice a week. Neither his medical insurance nor Medicare covered much of the costs, so he was spending the bulk of his income —and gradually eating up his life savings—in order to stay alive.

But his daughter, and her husband, had other uses for the money. They had sued him, contending that he was mentally incompetent to handle his own money. They had persuaded the court to give them control of the finances, and the first thing they had done was to discontinue the costly dialysis treatments!

This poor man begged me for help. He was sure that he would die within ten days if he did not receive his treatments.

I organized an immediate campaign. I wrote an urgent Mailgram to the new President, Jimmy Carter, and persuaded many of my friends in National Right to Life to do the same. But our pleas went unanswered.

The man was wrong. He did not die after ten days without treatment. He died on the twelfth day.

This is one of the most flagrant and despicable cases of what I call active euthanasia, the terrifying practice of giving someone the right to determine whether or not someone else should live or die. I am terrified that it will occur increasingly in the future.

It was Adolf Hitler who coined the term "useless eaters" to describe people whom he considered to be a drag upon society. He began to slaughter individuals who were brain-damaged, retarded, senile, and schizophrenic. Only then did he extend his murderous campaign to the Jews and other groups.

There are those in our society today who would do the same. Make no mistake about it. There is a conspiracy in America today to get rid of "useless eaters" and who knows where it will end?

Consider this: Officials of the American Medical Association should be arrested as accessories after the fact to murder. They printed the evidence against themselves in their own publication, *The Journal of the American Medical Association,* on January 8, 1988, in the form of a letter written by a doctor. I call it "Debbie Does Death," and it is, if anything, even more pornographic than the famous sex film with a similar name. It is worth quoting at length, but it makes me so angry

that I must interrupt it with my own comments. The
letter began:

*The call came in the middle of the night. As a gyne-
cology resident rotating through a large private hospital, I had come to detest telephone calls, because in-
variably I would be up for several hours and would not
feel good the next day. However, duty called, so I answered the phone . . .*

Here is a doctor, a member of the profession that
longs to be revered for its contributions to life, liberty,
and the pursuit of happiness, who begins his murder
confession by telling us how he hates to be disturbed
from his innocent slumber simply because a patient
needs him. This doctor complains that he will not feel
good the next day. If I did what he is about to do, I
would not feel good either.

Here is what confronts him:

*. . . a twenty-year-old girl named Debbie was dying
of ovarian cancer. . . . Hmmm, I thought . . . A second woman, also dark-haired but of middle age, stood
at her right, holding her hand. Both looked up as I entered. The room seemed filled with the patient's desperate effort to survive . . .*

The doctor has just made a critical admission. Despite stumbling around through the fog of his inter-
rupted sleep, he is astute enough to realize instantly
that Debbie is trying to remain alive. She is making a
"desperate effort to survive." He describes the horrors
of her plight, and calls it:

*. . . a gallows scene, a cruel mockery of her youth
and unfulfilled potential. Her only words to me were,
"Let's get this over with" . . .*

Here is a sudden change of diagnosis. Can the doctor
be sure? Is Debbie making a determined effort to survive or a determined effort not to survive? In his wis-

dom, so says the doctor, he could discern the truth—and the truth called for *20 mg. of morphine sulfate.* Suddenly the doctor, not God, held in his hands the power of life and death.

I took the syringe into the room and told the two women I was going to give Debbie something that would let her rest and to say good-bye.

Debbie looked at the syringe, then laid her head on the pillow with her eyes open, watching what was left of the world. I injected the morphine intravenously and watched to see if my calculations on its effects would be correct. Within seconds her breathing slowed to a normal rate, her eyes closed, and her features softened as she seemed restful at last. The older woman stroked the hair of the now-sleeping patient. I waited for the inevitable next effect of depressing the respiratory drive. With clocklike certainty, within four minutes the breathing rate slowed even more, then became irregular, then ceased. The dark-haired woman stood erect and seemed relieved.

It's over, Debbie.

Now, maybe the overworked doctor can get a good night's sleep.

All of this is bad enough, a case of murder, pure and simple, just as surely as if he had bludgeoned her to death. But the felony is compounded by the final line:

Name withheld by request.

Thus far have we progressed in our disdain for the sanctity of human life that we have the *Journal of the American Medical Association* printing the story of a murder and withholding the name of the murderer. There is complicity on the part of the editors, after the fact, unless they release the name of that murderer, that self-righteous doctor who had no right to make the determination that it was time for Debbie to die. That is a determination that only God can make.

In this country we are already practicing euthanasia, or perhaps it is more accurate to say that we are authorizing suicide. We allow people to determine, in some respects, the mode and moment of their death. We have even coined a catchy phrase, "Death with Dignity."

We call it death with dignity when we remove the intravenous feeding tube from a human being whose existence we have written off. It then takes from one to three weeks for the person to starve and dehydrate. Dignity, my ass!

Doctors have gone a long way to convince us that someone is dead when they have been diagnosed as "brain dead." Who makes the diagnosis? Doctors, of course. And they may make that determination upon the basis of any one of about thirty definitions, most of which do not require them to administer an electroencephalograph to determine if there is any brain wave activity.

Is there room here for abuse?

Ask the man in St. Louis who managed to blink an eye just before doctors were ready to kill him in order to use his liver for a transplant operation.

Ask the New Jersey man whose obituary ran in the newspaper after doctors diagnosed him as brain dead, but who is today a truck driver. Who could blame him if he ran his truck over one of those doctors who tried to kill him?

Ask Becky Maitz, who fell from the back of a truck in 1985. Doctors at Princeton University Hospital told her mother, Veronica Hyatt, that Becky was brain dead and was going to die. Mrs. Hyatt visited the hospital chapel for a few minutes and said, "Like hell she is."

She moved Becky to another hospital where other doctors saved her. Today, twenty-one-year-old Becky is happily married.

Put your life into the hands of others and you better believe there will be abuse. Doctors would have you ignore Dylan Thomas's sage advice, "Do not go gentle into that good night." I, like the poet, would prefer to go out kicking and screaming, but if present trends continue neither you nor I may have that choice.

What bothers me most about so-called passive euthanasia is that it is one step removed from active euthanasia. Today you can legally create a document known as a "living will," which states that it is your desire not to be kept alive by extraordinary means, if there appears to be no hope of recovery. To me, that "living will" is a dangerous and murky middle ground between making your own decision to surrender to death and giving someone else the authority to murder you. In a codicil of your "living will" you can designate a relative or friend whom you trust to make the proper, compassionate decision. If you sign such a document, you are giving over control of your very existence to someone else, and this is the first step toward the type of genocide perpetrated by Adolf Hitler.

A few years ago, on my NBC radio show originating from Chicago, I had as a guest a young woman who had remained in a coma for six months. During that time, her mother asked a judge to let her die, contending that this had been the girl's stated wish, should she ever be the victim of an apparently irreversible coma. Fortunately the judge refused. The young woman recovered and sued her mother for damages; she had *never* expressed a desire to have the plug pulled.

Unless we change the trend, I suspect that the day will come when doctors and public officials, in their

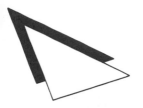

godlike wisdom, will declare when you ought to die. Even now we hear such proclamations, floated as trial balloons. Richard Lamm, when he was governor of Colorado, declared that old people had "a duty to die" and stop being a burden to the productive young.

This is what Orwell meant when he warned that political rhetoric could make murder a merciful act.

Way back in 1978 I stumped the world, speaking to concerned groups in Australia, New Zealand, and the Philippines. My primary target was a group called the Hemlock Society, which advocated "death with dignity," mercy killing and suicide. It was my contention a decade ago that once the pabulum-pukers convince us that we have the right to take our own lives, they will then move on to the next logical step, contending that the government has the right to take our lives. I predicted that supposedly brilliant thinkers would determine that society would have the right to remove those individuals who were not making a "meaningful contribution."

If that horrible reality should come about, who will determine what a "meaningful contribution" is? Is it not a meaningful contribution for a grandmother to visit with her grandchildren and tell them about the adventures she had in growing up, to tell them of the beauty—and the ugliness—in the world? Will some doctor or judge or jury or politician declare that if you are earning less than the average income, you are not making a "meaningful contribution"?

The answer may well be yes. One of the most frightening and dangerous guests to appear on my television show was Daniel Callahan, Ph.D., of the Hastings Institute, a "think-tank" devoted to the study of so-called medical ethics. Dr. Callahan provides evidence that the words "medical ethics" are a contradiction in terms.

Here is a fair summary of what he said: The current use of high-technology lifesaving procedures "costs us a great deal of money." By spending so much money to keep old people alive, we will "do harm to other age groups and other social needs." Therefore, we should stop paying big bucks to keep old people alive.

Dr. Callahan says he is not a believer in euthanasia or suicide. He says he does not want the government to kill people; he merely wants the government to say that human life can reach a point where Medicare should no longer foot the bill for life-extending technologies. And what is that point? "I think we will have to use age as the cut-off point," he declares.

Look at that one closely, gang. This expert in "medical ethics" is not saying that we should kill old people. What he really is saying is that we should kill old *poor* people. If we cut off Medicare support at a certain age, the poor people will die and the rich people will pay for the care themselves. This line of logic may have a certain appeal to those with money, such as politicians, lawyers, and . . . of course . . . doctors, but what do *you* think about it?

When I called Dr. Callahan a Nazi, he seemed offended.

But he is setting the stage for the same sort of evil promoted by Adolf Hitler. This is the same sort of crap that population experts are fond of spouting. Dr. Callahan wants to set the limit at about eighty years of age. After that point, Medicare will pay nickels and dimes to relieve your pain, but that is about all. In his book, *Setting Limits,* he declares: "Pneumonia should be allowed to become an old man's best friend."

What if he is successful in selling this sugar-coated

cyanide pill to the nation? Set the limit at eighty years old and the next jerk who interprets the law will say it should be seventy and then some other bubble-head will come along and try to lower it to sixty.

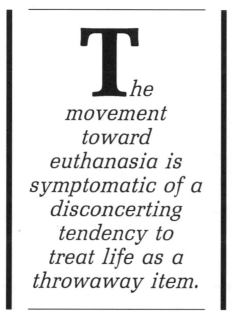

The movement toward euthanasia is symptomatic of a disconcerting tendency to treat life as a throwaway item.

Given the current state of erosion of the sacred value of life, it is not farfetched to envision a future wherein, when you reach a predetermined age, you are given ninety days to determine how you will die. You can go to a "Death with Dignity" center, watch television, eat pies and cakes, and meet wonderful new friends with whom you can play cards. Then, one by one, the foursome will disappear from your bridge table.

We see the signs of such coldhearted society all about us today. Dr. Callahan says he is "impressed" by the system already in use in Great Britain, where there are not enough kidney dialysis machines to go around. If you are a Britisher suffering from kidney disease, and you are unlucky enough to be past the magic age of fifty-five, you will not be given dialysis. You are sentenced to die. This is far more than ridiculous; it is absolutely criminal. I *am* fifty-five, and no one is going to croak me. Under this sort of system, President Reagan might have been refused surgery for colon cancer.

We live in a technological era. We can build aircraft carriers, submarines, long-range bombers, and enough missiles to kill us all many times over in one great wave of collective euthanasia. Why can we not build enough dialysis machines?

One answer comes to mind and it is truly frightening. The past twenty years have seen a steady erosion of morality within the leadership of the medical profession. The American Medical Association, for example, supports abortion on demand. The doctor-politicians who control the profession have led their followers down an evil garden path, taught them to disrespect the sanctity of life, and cheapened it even for those of us who remain alive in spite of the doctors.

The movement toward euthanasia is symptomatic of a disconcerting tendency to treat life as a throwaway item. If a human being is no longer of any use to you, throw him out. We are already doing this when we force a fifty-five-year-old man to take early retirement. We spit in the face of his experience on the job and, indeed, in life.

Dr. Callahan's theory has one glaring practical fault far removed from its ghastly spiritual faults. He assumes that the government wants to save money when we all know that, in truth, the government only *says* it wants to save money. The only way to maintain government as a vigorous growth industry is to create new programs to spend more of our tax dollars. I will bow both to reality and rhetoric and suggest two solutions, one that involves spending money and one that seeks to save it.

If the government is so all-fired anxious to spend money, let it create a workforce of all those people who were retired against their will. Integrate them into a labor force to rebuild and revitalize the infrastructure of America. Let them rebuild the highways, bridges, and public buildings that are nearing collapse. Just issue a call to what we euphemistically call the "golden agers." Do you want to sit around twiddling your thumbs or do you want to rebuild America? You will have an army of willing workers on your hands and they will be loaded with the precious commodity of experience.

Put them to work if you can.

Let them sit if you must.

But in the name of human dignity, do not kill them.

There is, in fact, a way to make old age far happier and healthier than it is today, and save a bundle of tax dollars at the same time.

Consider this:

If you are a doctor in this country today, you have benefited from several of the government's multitudinous handouts (just as if you were a lawyer). Your medical school received federal money to supplement the cost of your education. Chances are you borrowed a considerable amount of money under federally-insured student

Require *every doctor in America to donate 25 percent of his time to provide* free *medical care for anyone over 80.*

loan programs. In your practice today, you may well receive a major portion of your income from Medicare and Medicaid. The medicine you prescribe and the extraordinary technologies you utilize were developed in large measure out of the $1-billion annual budget of the National Institutes of Health. Hear this, Doctor, and hear it well: The people paid for your education and your practice and it is about time you returned some interest on that debt.

Where is it written that doctors should earn so much money, trading upon human misery? Who said doctors have an inalienable right to a Mercedes-Benz and a country club membership?

In this country today, there are fewer than six hundred gerontologists—doctors who specialize in the care of the elderly. Why? Because the elderly cannot finance the Mercedes and the country club membership, that's why.

Here is a simple answer to the problem: Make every doctor be a gerontologist. Require every doctor in America to donate 25 percent of his or her time to provide *free* medical care for anyone over eighty. Then lower the age to seventy, then sixty. No longer would we have to worry about the impact of Medicare upon the federal budget deficit.

Perhaps the most beautiful person ever to step up to one of my Loudmouth podiums and air an opinion was Julie Reed, a gentle-looking "young lady" who described herself as "going on seventy-one." She looked squarely at Dr. Callahan, but she addressed her comments to anyone with a spark of human decency, and as she spoke, her aging voice took on increasing strength. She said: "My generation saw to it that Dr. Callahan's generation could be here. My generation saw to it that Dr. Callahan would not be enslaved by the Japanese and Germans and the Italians who declared war on this country. Two hundred ninety-two thousand one hundred thirty-one of our men and some of our women—one hundred eighty-one of our women —lie in the Pacific and Atlantic and Arctic oceans and in the real estate of the Pacific and North Africa and in Europe. And they died so that you could be here to-night. And as the Germans came toward our men with guns, our men did not set limits!"

There is, in this country, and in this world, a multi-tude of competent and caring physicians who remain true to the noble ideals of medicine and its first basic tenet, *Do no harm!* Many of them, in fact, now refuse to be members of the American Medical Association (non-membership, by the way, is one of the finest crite-ria I can think of for selecting a competent physician). It is the leadership of the medical establishment that has undermined the value of life and it is time for new leadership. Just as we all need a new set of leaders in our government, so, too, does the medical community.

Doctors used to take pride in their Hippocratic Oath. Perhaps they should reread the words of Hippocrates, which are clear enough:

The regimen I adopt shall be for the benefit of my patients according to my ability and judgment, and not for their hurt or for any wrong. I will give no deadly drugs to any, though it be asked of me, nor will I coun-sel such . . .

But American doctors are no longer required to take the Hippocratic Oath. I wonder why? Is it because they have replaced it with their own hypocritic ideology, with which they would usurp the very powers of God?

I don't know how I will leave this world, but if I had my druthers, I would die at the age of ninety-seven, beaten up by a jealous husband.

Twenty years ago I wrote words of prophecy, words that spoke to this ghastly issue. When I wrote them, I was unaware consciously of the import they would carry today, but the right side of my brain must have been able to peer into a dismal future. I said this, twenty years ago, to the Dr. Callahans of the world:

God help you, blind man,
With eyes that see
But cannot cry.
How foolish you are,
You too must die.

5

Abortion

In THE PREVIOUS CHAPTER I LEFT OFF THE final portion of the quote from Hippocrates, saving it for this topic. Hippocrates added: ". . . and especially, I will not aid a woman to procure abortion." I know a man who found himself, as a layman, bound by that same oath.

He married a young woman in a fit of anger after his parents objected to his seeing her. He and his bride slept together on their honeymoon night, and never again.

However, the miracle of nature was operative and the wife became pregnant.

The wife, however, did not wish to have the baby. She began to take extended hot baths. Several times she jumped from furniture onto the floor, trying to jar the fetus from her womb.

My friend grew increasingly alarmed that she would succeed, so he told her a solemn lie: "I have some friends who know how to take care of this. I'll get you something." He whipped up a crazy concoction of wheat germ and vitamins, and assured her that it would dissolve the baby. This, at least, stopped her from jumping off of the dresser until the pregnancy had reached the point of no return. Finally a lovely daughter was born to the couple.

In the early 1970s, I myself confronted the issue of unwanted pregnancy. When Washington State passed a law allowing abortion on demand, and when the Supreme Court upheld it, I found I could not stand on the sidelines.

I heard feminists proclaim that unwanted pregnancies were holding women back from full participation in economic life.

I heard population-control experts assert that the world was being strained beyond capacity, and I recognized that fraudulent line of reasoning. The United States has already achieved zero population growth, so there is no need to kill off more babies within our borders. Sure, population growth is out of control in many third-world countries, but there is precedent for dealing with the problem. God has always maintained control of the population through famine, pestilence, disease, and war, and I, for one, see no reason to usurp His control over the issue of who will live and who will die.

In combination with the well-meaning, perhaps, feminists and population-control experts, there arose the leaders of the medical community, who were willing and able to support a lucrative new form of business. Most abortion laws were written in a two-tiered structure. During the first trimester of pregnancy, the mother alone could make the decision whether or not to abort. During the second trimester she had to have the acquiescence of one or two doctors, and every abortion chamber in the United States is operated by at least two doctors who would willingly cooperate. Very quickly abortion became big business.

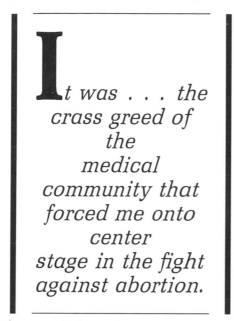

It was . . . the crass greed of the medical community that forced me onto center stage in the fight against abortion.

It was this latter point that obsessed me the most. Yes, I am morally and adamantly opposed to abortion and I will argue my position with anyone who cares to listen. But I am hesitant to attempt to impose my morals upon someone else. Someday, somewhere, you and I will stand before the same God and we can answer then and there for our own moral decisions. It was, however, the crass greed of the medical community that forced me onto center stage in the fight against abortion. I became a lobbyist for the National Right to Life Movement and chairman of the Life Amendment for Local Action Committee, the political action arm of NRLM. As a born loudmouth, I was soon recognized as one of the most vehement antiabortion spokespersons.

I would not have been so angry if doctors had been more open and honest with their patients. Abortionists made little effort to explain the effects of the procedure upon either the mother or the fetus, and they consistently failed to detail the alternatives, such as adoption.

In 1978, I put them to the test. I wired my fourteen-year-old daughter Tracey with a hidden microphone and sent her into a Planned Parenthood office in Reno, Nevada. She told the case officer that she had missed her period two months in a row.

"Well, my dear, you will ruin your life if you have a baby", the woman said. "You should have an abortion."

My daughter played her part well. She asked, "How will I tell my father?"

The woman from Planned Parenthood explained, "You don't have to tell your father. The Supreme Court has said that your parents do not have to know."

"I don't believe that," Tracey replied. "When I wanted to get my ears pierced, they made me bring a note from my father!"

"This is different. The Supreme Court says you don't need a note from your father."

"How much does it cost?"

"Well, we don't perform the abortions here. We send you down to the Westside Clinic. It will be about $175. You better bring cash."

All of this transpired on the assumption that she was pregnant, because she said her period was two months late. The woman gave my daughter an empty bottle and told her to take a urine sample to the clinic the following day.

Sure enough, the tests proved that Tracey was pregnant, the abortion doctors never suspecting that the yellow fluid they tested was urine collected from Seanie, our male Lhasa apso dog!

Tracey and I told that story, with our tapes as evidence, to a committee of the Nevada State Senate that was considering a bill to fund Planned Parenthood in Nevada. After our testimony those funds were denied.

I still worry that, like my daughter, many girls are misdiagnosed as pregnant, and that many of them are actually given "abortions." I worry that abortion has already become such a huge, entrenched business that it will never be wiped out.

The woman from Planned Parenthood made a telling statement on our tapes. After she had assumed that Tracey was pregnant and endeavored to talk her into having an abortion, she referred to the supposed contents of Tracey's womb, not as a child, or a baby, or a fetus, but merely as "the residue of your last period." What a horrible, inhuman description for a collection of human cells, tiny and defenseless, to be sure, that already had a beating heart.

I am not a theologian. I believe that only God knows the moment when life begins. I would not care to substitute *my* judgment for His. But believing in God, I would not wish to take the slightest chance that an unborn fetus, no matter how young, did not possess a soul.

What if we kill off the one person who might be able to design a treaty that would allow the world to live in lasting peace? Or cure AIDS or cancer or heart disease? Or find a viable way to eliminate poverty, hunger, and homelessness?

Suppose there had been abortion clinics two thousand years ago, readily available to young unwed women who did not have to tell their parents? We might have aborted the Messiah!

6

Drugs

W<small>HY DO YOU THINK THEY CALL IT</small> *SHIT?*
I was living in Dayton, Ohio, for a time, still determined to make it on my own as a disc jockey, without
help from my father. I held down the 9 A.M. to noon slot
on WONE as Morton Downey, Jr., and the 9 P.M. to
midnight slot as Doctor D. There was a young woman
named Toni, whom I befriended, and before long we
were living together.

Toni was a high-energy person who complained that
my two jobs sapped my strength. To build up my energy level, she said, I should take vitamins. She handed
me a little white pill and said, "This is vitamin A. Take
it."

I did, and within half an hour I thought I could feel
the effects. I *did* have more energy.

So I began to take Toni's vitamin A pills regularly. I
started with one pill a day and, before I knew it, I was
taking six. I enjoyed them so much that, by the time

Toni went on vacation to visit friends in California, I made sure she left me a supply. After she had been gone for a few days, she called to say she was extending the visit a bit longer. My first thought was for my supply of vitamin pills. I had only one left. I forced myself to save it, so that I could show it to my pharmacist and get a supply exactly like it.

This turned into a difficult evening. I grew steadily more irritable, restless, and even nauseated. I stared at the little white pill and had to muster my resolve not to swallow it.

By the next morning I felt truly horrible. My head was pounding. My nerves were raw. To make matters worse, my apartment was over the local firehouse; whenever the damn siren went off I thought my head would burst. I called my boss and told him I was ill. Then, somehow, I got dressed, grabbed my remaining vitamin A pill, and crawled out to a drugstore. I happened to know the pharmacist, a guy named Phil.

"I don't know what kind of a pill this is," I said. "It's vitamin A or something like that, and it gives me great energy. Can you look in your book, find out what it is, and give me some?"

"It's not any vitamin that I've ever seen," Phil mumbled. He studied his book for a while, then came back to me and announced, "This isn't a vitamin. This is speed."

"What the hell is speed?"

"An amphetamine. A diet pill," he said. "It certainly *would* give you more energy."

"Can you give me some?" I pleaded.

"No! You have to have a doctor's prescription for this. Can you get one?"

"I don't have a doctor here in town," I said.

"Well, Mort, I can't give it to you. This stuff is pretty

illegal." Phil studied my face and saw bloodshot eyes. Sweat was pouring off of me. "How long have you been taking this?" he asked.

"About two months."

"Jesus!" he exclaimed. "Look, pal, you're hooked. You'd better get off these fast."

Back in my apartment, I locked myself inside. I knew that I had to stay there and suffer the consequences of my gullibility. I had to get the drugs out of my system.

The next forty-eight hours were a blur. I spent most of the time crying, sweating, vomiting, throwing things around the apartment, and calling Toni a bitch at the top of my lungs.

The second morning I woke up feeling weak, but better; I knew the worst was over. I had lost nine pounds in two days but I had kicked the speed.

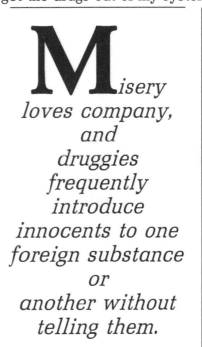

Misery loves company, and druggies frequently introduce innocents to one foreign substance or another without telling them.

Toni came back on the third day, and the moment when she walked through the door was the closest I have ever come to beating up a woman. She had committed what I later learned to be a very common sin within the drug subculture. Misery loves company, and druggies frequently introduce innocents to one foreign substance or another without telling them.

From that day on, I have never even taken an aspirin unless I personally removed it from the bottle.

I am convinced that some substance in illegal drugs suppresses the natural human instinct to tell the truth. Drugs distort one's perception of reality, and reality is truth. Under the influence of drugs, a person begins to toy with reality; truth becomes a very relative concept.

This may be a more dangerous side effect than the actual physical results. Truth is all we have, gang. We have already strayed too far from it, and if we go much further, we will be lost.

Perhaps politicians suffer from the same effect induced by power, for they tend to stray far from the truth when they proclaim how they are making inroads against drug trafficking. If we are, as they declare, waging a war on drugs, then we are fighting somewhat less effectively than we did in Vietnam. Both proponents and critics of the Vietnam war agree on one thing: If we were going to fight, we should have kept the politicians away from it and allowed our military to go in and get the job done. Vietnam gave us a clear example of the stupidity of waging war in a namby-pamby fashion, yet we are doubling the error in our so-called war on drugs.

Suppose you were an American soldier in Vietnam and you saw a Vietcong troop kill your best buddy. You manage to capture the enemy soldier. Then what happens? He is turned over to pabulum-puking psychiatrists who spend six weeks "rehabilitating" him, then set him free in the jungle and tell him not to do it again! What do you suppose you might do the next time you catch that man killing one of your friends?

Even in Vietnam we weren't *that* stupid, yet that is exactly how we are fighting the "war" on drugs. Can you believe it?

If we are going to win this new war, we had better get serious about fighting it. We've got to develop more compassion for the victims and get rid of every iota of compassion for the enemy.

We need to establish levels of guilt, and to me, there is a clear line of demarcation. Why anyone would be dumb enough to allow someone to control his brain and body is a mystery to me, but why they would willingly remove themselves from reality is a greater one. You can avoid reality for a time, but sooner or later it will slam its fist into your face. Perhaps it is tied inextricably to the fact that too many people see ahead of them a dismal reality of dependency and depression, with no visible means of working to improve their lot. Especially on the street, the temptation must be great to avoid reality as long as possible—and there is every manner of lowlife around to provide the means.

Here is the clear line of demarcation. Treat the user as a victim, not a perpetrator—unless and until he becomes even a small cog in the distribution system.

Drug use creates an extremely vicious cycle. The user moves further and further away from truth. He drops his moral guard by degrees. What starts as self-abuse soon is extended to others. The addict is simply unhappy to be alone in his slime pit. He must draw others into his deadly world. Once he has reached that point, I believe he has forfeited the right to our sympathy.

I am not sure whether or not you have the legal and moral right to kill yourself via suicide, or by signing a "living will," but I'm damn sure you don't have the right to kill anyone else. If you cross that line, in my mind, you cannot return.

We have seen enough of drug abuse to know that it is contagious. If you are diagnosed with cholera, bu-

bonic plague, or leprosy, society has the right to quar-
antine you for the protection of others. It should have
the same right when it identifies the drug user. For the
simple user, this should take the form of an enlightened
punishment. We are not punishing the user so much as
we are quarantining him. We have caught him at, we
hope, an early stage of infection, and we hope to cur-
tail that infection before it spreads. Send him to a
rehab center. Pile on the community service work—
lots of it. Henceforth, make him undergo periodic urine
testing. But whatever you do, do not send him to a
prison where he will have even more need to escape
from reality and where he may find it even easier to get
drugs. In sum, treat him with love and compassion, and
with the stern bearing of a parent who says, "Okay,
you've made a mistake. We will give you a second
chance." Make it clear, however, that there will be no
third chance.

This approach will save some individuals. I am cynical enough about drugs, however, to believe that no
amount of rehab and psychiatric counseling will work
until we adopt a far more hard-hearted attitude toward
anyone who distributes illegal drugs to another—in
any way, shape, or form. The only way to get drugs off
the street is to get drug dealers off the street. Let them
know: *If you are caught selling, you are gone, baby!*
And I mean, you are gone for as long as it takes to
bring back the life of someone you may have killed
with that drug.

Now, let's take it further. The street-seller of drugs is
most often a user himself. He sells in order to support
his own habit. This does not excuse him—other people
grill hamburgers at Wendy's all day to pay their living
expenses—but it does suggest that he is sufficiently removed from the voice of his own conscience that I find

a tiny measure of sympathy in my heart. Forget about rehabilitating him, for he has identified himself as the carrier of a deadly virus. Lock him up and throw away the key. Let him rot. Maybe he will serve as an example to society—maybe not. But at least he will be off the streets.

There is a third level to the drug trade that deserves our greatest scorn and most severe punishment. The major distributor and importer is often not a drug user himself. He is, rather, the lowest form of economic scum. Think up the filthiest stream of obscenities you can, insert them here: ——, ——, ——, ——, and your description will be inadequate. These are people who trade in human degradation and misery, who will torture, maim, enslave, and murder for the single objective of money.

How can we countenance them? How can we entertain the slightest possibility that, once caught, they will ever again walk free? March them to the electric chair and say, "Sit down, pal. Get ready for the ultimate high."

There is a specious argument going around. It declares that the moment we bust up one drug ring, others will take its place. The implication is, why bother? If you fall for that one, you might as well take a quick overdose yourself, for you have come to believe that we cannot make things better than they are. Every drug dealer out of circulation is a victory. Never lose sight of the fact that the majority of the world's population are good guys and gals. We *can* win, if we fight the war the way it should be fought.

We must escalate it so that we train our biggest guns all the way down to the origin of the deadly pipeline. The number one cash crop in California today is marijuana. If we can defoliate millions of acres of Vietnam, surely we can burn out California's marijuana crop.

We could, and should, do the same elsewhere in the world. Our government officials do not want to say so, but the fact is that several nations of the world are at war with us. These include Colombia, Mexico, and Thailand. At the moment I reserve judgment against Thailand, for officials there appear to be making attempts to clean up their act. But Colombia and Mexico are exporting death to our American streets. They are killing our citizens, just as surely as the Vietcong did. Is this not an act of war?

Did we, during the Vietnam war, send billions of dollars in aid to Hanoi? Of course not. The American people would have lynched any government official who sanctioned that. Why, then, do we continue aiding countries who are killing our people? Why send them a penny?

Countries like Colombia and Mexico . . . owe our banks billions of dollars.

Because, gang, countries like Colombia and Mexico are holding us hostage. They already owe our banks billions of dollars in loans that they cannot pay back in the foreseeable future. That money came, by the way, not from the government's tax revenues, but from our very own savings accounts. The bankers are running scared, and our government kowtows to their wishes, so that their already shaky loans are not put in further jeopardy.

Does this make the bankers drug importers? You bet it does.

Do they deserve the same fate as other drug importers? You bet they do.

Corrupted foreign governments are going to continue to allow the export of deadly drugs just as long as they can

Does this make the bankers drug importers? You bet it does.

make a buck—or a peso—in doing so. The answer is to hit them where it hurts. Cut off all aid. Send them nothing. *No más!*

If that does not work, take the next logical step. Give these merchants of death a taste of what napalm and Agent Orange can do to their fields of hemp and poppies.

In contrast to Vietnam, it would stand as one of the most easily justifiable wars ever waged.

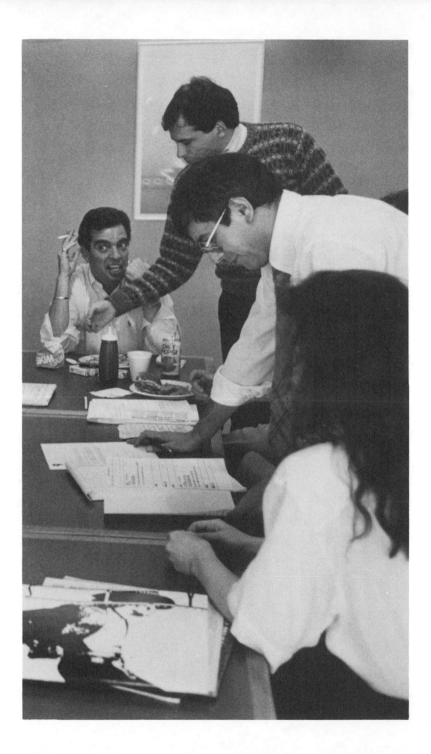

7
Race

SHOW ME A LIBERAL AND I'LL SHOW YOU A
racist.

If you call him that, he will deny it to the death, of
course, and therein lies the problem. The liberal is a
blind racist; he does not even recognize his own prejudice.

It took years of tumult for me to realize this. I ran a
rocky emotional gauntlet, confused, not about my basic attitudes toward race relations, but about the solutions to the problems.

I am a member of a race that suffered great prejudice
in America, and even today suffers and dies in its
homeland at the hands of the British. There were Irish
ghettos in Boston when my father was a boy. Rarely
did I personally feel the effects, for my Irish family was
prosperous and privileged, as were our neighbors in
Hyannisport, the Kennedys. I played baseball on the

lawn of the Kennedy home with Jack, Bob, Teddy, and their sisters, Pat and Jean.

Looking back, it seems to me that the Kennedy boys, with the possible exception of Bobby, grew up with a guilt complex about how their father had made his fortune. As a result they had a burning desire to take care of the poor. Their motives were wonderful, but over the years, as I saw their solutions put into place—and fail —I came to see them as typifiers of the liberals too blind to see their own prejudice.

There were numerous black people living in our home, but they were confined to the servants' areas. I often hung out in the kitchen with them and, somehow, I knew that they were disadvantaged. For some reason life did not seem to present them with the same opportunities that it did me.

When, against my father's wishes, I launched my own singing career, I entered a different sort of world, where the color of one's skin was simply unimportant. Sound mattered; color did not. When I signed to record for a label called Stax Records, I was the only white artist under contract to them. No one in this world was afraid to say the word "nigger," because everyone said it. It was a term that could be applied with venom, yes, but also with affection—sort of like the word "mother" today.

In the dim light of a honky-tonk, few people worried about the color of a musician's skin. Talent was the great equalizer. But sometimes, when we emerged into the bright light of day, my friends and I were rudely reminded that some people in the world considered us different due to an accident of pigmentation.

One day I walked into a restaurant in Tuscaloosa, Alabama, with Fats Domino. The white man behind the counter said, "We don't serve niggers here."

Fats replied, "I don't want a nigger. I want a hamburger."

I thought his joke was funny until the white man told me I could stay, but Fats had to leave. I could not understand. Fats's skin was a different color, and he spoke with a different accent than I did, but he was a human being. He had a family he loved, people he cared for, a trade he was plying. Most important, he was my friend. So I stormed out of the restaurant with him, with the beginnings of a realization that I had to work with my friends to bring about change. I did not do it out of a sense of guilt, like the Kennedys, or because my great-grandpappy may have had slaves on his plantation, or even out of a sense of altruism for the entire black race. My friends were hurt. That's why I did it.

So I became involved in the early civil rights marches in the late fifties, viewing myself as a quiet liberal. I was a follower, not a leader, marching in Atlanta, marching in Columbia, South Carolina, marching in Selma, Alabama. I was arrested a few times and brought into the police station, but never detained for long, never treated rudely. The moments of confrontation were tense, trying, and riveting but, all in all, not as openly hostile as the press sometimes portrayed. We were simply a group of friends asserting our basic Constitutional rights.

One of those friends was the Reverend Jesse Jackson. We first met when he recorded his "Country Preacher" album for Stax Records, and our friendship deepened as we worked together for civil rights. I even helped him write some speeches. I still speak with Jesse, perhaps twice a year. We remain good friends, and we retain many of the same basic goals, but we differ on tactics.

Actually, way back in the fifties, I saw President Eisenhower blow a golden opportunity to meld this country together once and for all, so that we would never again have problems uniting the whites, blacks, and Hispanics in their common goals as an American society. During the time when the government and the courts were struggling with the problems associated with school integration, President Eisenhower could have decreed that every kindergarten in the country would be fully integrated; the next year every first grade would be fully integrated, and so on. Thirteen years later the nation would have been integrated, and it would have happened at the roots. This would have brought fierce opposition from many parents, both in the South and in northern cities where racism is alive and well but less acknowledged. Yet I believe it could have worked. If President Eisenhower would have attacked racism as tenaciously as General Eisenhower attacked Nazism, he could have destroyed two evils. It was not to be, however. The liberals found different "solutions."

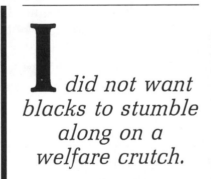

I *did not want blacks to stumble along on a welfare crutch.*

Even in the early days I felt no compulsion to give black people what I already had. My goal was to see that they had the opportunity to go out and work for their own success. I did not want blacks to stumble along on a welfare crutch, and I do not believe that the great majority of blacks wanted that either.

Over the years I saw our noble goals subverted,

often by well-meaning people. I saw numerous solutions attempted, and these mostly boiled down to throwing money at blacks. This did little to solve the underlying problem of prejudice and, indeed, made it worse. Some blacks became more angry than ever, and I responded with an emotional backlash. I found resentment growing within me when a black would tell me how rotten white people were.

One night I walked into a club where a friend of mine, a black man named Plas Gresham, was playing sax. He was well known within the recording industry, having played with The Coasters and other top rock 'n' roll groups. During his break, he came over to the table and sat down. He glanced around at the club filled with white people and said, "Well, I see we've got whitey listening to blackie's music." Then he launched a diatribe about how whites had done nothing for blacks, and how he could have been further ahead in his career if only he had been white.

It was too much. I said, "Hey, let me ask you something, pal. What are you earning here?"

"I'm earning $1,250 a week," he grumbled. "If I was white, I'd be a superstar and I'd be earning $5,000 a week."

I said, "If you were earning $5,000 a week, it would be white people paying you the money. There are no blacks in here! If you are such a great black player, where are the blacks? You're earning this money because of whites. The whites are the ones supporting your talent."

Plas could not seem to understand my point, nor I his. We had both become embittered and disillusioned. Why?

I saw the same bitterness in other former friends. Ernie Freeman, one of the great songwriters of his day, who wrote for Ricky Nelson, Glen Campbell, and others, lost his driver's license after his fifth citation for driving under the influence, and became very embittered at the white policemen who had nabbed him. Even when I reminded him that, through a friend, I got three of those tickets buried, he would not acknowledge his own irresponsibility for drinking and driving.

I could understand the bitterness of my black friends toward fate, toward prejudice, toward a system that still, in many ways, discriminated against them. But I could not understand their bitterness toward me. In the early days we had tried to take that bitterness and turn it into a positive, forward motion. Somehow it had all turned negative. Why the hell did I go out and bust my butt? I asked myself. The world is not perfect, but we gave blacks a better chance than before, didn't we? Some of them have moved into the middle class, and even into the upper middle class, but the majority are still where they were thirty years ago. Why are so many black people still living in abject poverty?

I was on the verge of backlash. Black people no longer seemed interested in helping themselves, so why should I bother? It was then, after considerable thought, that the realization struck: It was the liberals who were racist, perhaps more so than any raving, redneck conservative. Sure, the liberals knew how to spout high-sounding rhetoric. Their motives were good, but their actions belied their true feelings.

The liberal solution to racial inequity had taken many forms, but boil them down and they all amount to this: "Throw money to the blacks; take care of them."

Why? Because, deep down inside, the liberals believed that blacks could not take care of themselves. They acted upon a conviction that blacks were not as

capable as whites and treated them almost as house-
hold pets.

The horrible result of this was the creation of a new
cottage industry in this country: poverty. I looked
around and I realized that a lot of people were getting
wealthy on poverty. And to keep that industry going,
you have to keep people in poverty, keep the blacks,
other minorities, and poor whites on welfare.

There is no way to separate the poverty issue from
the race issue. I became very upset to realize that we
have millions of people in this country who are not
being taught how to take care of themselves. We have
a government that feeds upon these people who get
into the welfare system and forces them to remain
there. We have created a form of economic slavery,
and we sit back and moan, "Look what we're doing for
these people, and they don't appreciate it."

We have become hypocrites. Long ago we should
have been willing to take the heat of the black leaders
and proclaim, *Enough is enough.*

We still have not freed the minorities of this country.
Equal rights protections are fine if you give someone
an equal opportunity to grab those rights—and an
equal opportunity to fail. If I am considering you for
admittance to Harvard University and I see that you
have a SAT score of 600, but I decide to let you in
anyway because you are a minority, I have ruined your
future. That is like signing a Little League baseball
player to the New York Yankees and expecting him to
function. It is a guaranteed ticket to failure. And depression, too, because I have told you that you have an
equal opportunity, so you should succeed. Yet you cannot possibly succeed *and I know it!* That makes me a
racist. No wonder my black friends grew bitter.

We've got to free black people and other minorities,

and the way to do that is to give them a truly equal opportunity to compete. Those who can compete on an equal footing should, indeed, be admitted to Harvard, but this is a pipe dream for the majority of young black men and women whom we have conditioned to live on welfare and whom we have further shackled by our joke of a public educational system. Education is the answer, but not when it puts the ambitious young person into a spot where he or she cannot maneuver. One sensible way to start would be to make sure that no American child, regardless of race, is passed through the school system unless he can read and write properly, balance a checkbook, and tie his shoelaces.

I believe firmly that the average minority man and woman in this country agree with me. But black and Hispanic leaders have lost touch with their own people, just as white leaders have. Here is a perfect example: Surveys show that 87 percent of black Americans are opposed to legalized abortion, but 89 percent of the black leadership is in favor of it. They are not dealing with reality. They are not addressing the concerns of their constituency. In that respect, at least, black politicians have achieved equality with their white counterparts.

One of the most insidious and perhaps *criminal* perversions of the fight for social equality is the Civil Rights Restoration Act of 1988, which, as of this writing, has been passed by Congress, vetoed by President Reagan, passed once again by Congress over the veto.

Congress says it is merely trying to close a loophole in the basic, historic Civil Rights Act, but in fact, it is using—and cruelly so—lofty rhetoric to once more disguise a lie. In theory, the law would prevent discrimination on the basis of race, sex, handicap, or age by any business, school, or other organization that accepts a dime of federal money—and that is a lofty goal.

In examining the law, however, let us first look at that *one and only* American institution that Congress chose to exempt from the law—Congress itself!

Congress is exempted from the provisions of Title VII of the Civil Rights Act, the Equal Pay Act, the National Labor Relations Act, the Age Discrimination Act, the Occupational Safety and Health Act, and of course, the Freedom of Information Act. The Congressional Black Caucus, which is funded by federal money, will not allow a white congressman to join.

For starters, therefore, the act is passed by hypocrites.

What they are doing is to create yet another vague umbrella of law, giving pabulum-puking judges broad powers of determination. For example, a Florida judge was confronted with a case involving a man who admittedly drank a pint of gin a day and had missed fourteen months of work in three years. When he was fired, he sued the company. The judge determined that, as an alcoholic, the man was handicapped and had been discriminated against. He awarded the drunk $150,000 in back pay!

More of the same absurdity is coming under the new law.

Are you handicapped if you are a transvestite, a kleptomaniac, or a pedophile? You sure are, buddy, but it is *not* a violation of your civil rights for me to fire you. It is a violation of *my* civil rights to be forced to keep you on the payroll.

No one stated it better than Michael Falkner of the National Black Coalition for Traditional Values when he said, "I don't want the sick and the sexual aberrant to be classified as minorities. The sexual aberrant chooses to live that way!"

Why is it that every perceived grievance has to be resolved by a blizzard of legislation? The so-called Civil Rights Restoration Act will restore nothing. Rather, it will simply create a new bureaucracy of 300,000 drones to attempt to administer it.

Look, gang, if you are a bigot, if you discriminate against anyone on the basis of race, national origin, sex, or religion, *you are scum.* But I don't need the damn government to write yet another law to tell me that.

What no one seems to acknowledge is that there is, in this country, a multitude of fair-minded people willing to accept anyone on an equal footing. This notion came through to me forcefully in 1969.

Two years earlier, while I was working to help organize the Ameri-

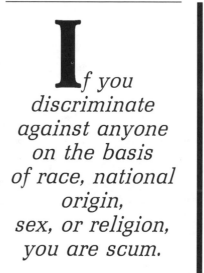

If you discriminate against anyone on the basis of race, national origin, sex, or religion, you are scum.

can Basketball Association and, at the same time, putting together my own team, the New Orleans Buccaneers, I walked into a New Orleans restaurant with one of my players, Marlbert Pradd, and his girlfriend. He was one of the finest young basketball players in the country, and he was black. The owner of the restaurant, who knew me, said, "Mort, you can come

in, but you have got to leave the nigger and his girlfriend outside."

He said this loud enough for Marlbert to hear. I
thought, *My God! How can you hurt someone whom
you don't even know?* I turned to Marlbert and said,
"Stand here, just a second. Don't get into any trouble.
I'll take care of this."

I went inside and walked straight to the bandstand. I
caught the eye of my friend Tommy Dawn, playing
there with his band, The Sunsets. "Tommy," I said,
"stop playing. I'm with a black friend and they won't
let us in the restaurant."

The band stopped playing immediately and packed
up its equipment.

"What the hell are you doing?" the manager
screamed.

"I know these guys," I said. "They don't like playing
in a restaurant where you won't let black people come
in."

Days later I was smacked with a half-million-dollar
lawsuit, filed by the restaurant owner, who claimed
that I had destroyed his business. It was two years
before the case came to trial, two years during which
the American Civil Liberties Union and every so-called
liberal lawyer in town refused to take the case. When I
walked into the courtroom in 1969 I had to represent
myself in a case with clear racial implications before a
jury of men and women from the Deep South. Luckily
they were my peers.

They had no difficulty in making a decision. Here
were twelve honest, middle-class men and women
who, given the opportunity, could separate right from
wrong. They ruled in my favor, against the restaurant
owner.

I say that these twelve southerners, like millions and

millions of their peers in America, are heroes who can break down the walls of prejudice through the application of common sense.

. . . if only their political leaders will let them.

Today's liberal looks down upon blacks and other minorities.

I am sick and tired of the liberals proclaiming that they are the only people in the country concerned about civil rights. That is an unadulterated lie. Today's liberal looks down upon blacks and other minorities. Whenever he says they cannot take care of themselves, he is exhibiting his hidden racism.

People cannot take care of themselves?

Baloney!!!

It is up to us to give them an equal opportunity to take care of themselves, then step aside to let them do it.

8
Education

> ▷

My DAUGHTER KELLI HAS ALWAYS BEEN A hard-working student. Thus I was surprised and dismayed when she began bringing home Ds in English. I spoke to her English teacher on the phone and suggested, "Challenge Kelli. Give her more homework. We'll see that she does it."

Kim and I both worked with Kelli on her homework. It was clear to me that her compositions were well written, neat, properly constructed and punctuated, and glistening with originality.

Still she brought home Ds.

"Dad, the teacher doesn't like me," she wailed.

"Well, honey, don't believe that. That's probably not true at all," I said.

Determined to find the answer to this perplexing problem, I penned a short note to the teacher. I wrote, "I have read Kelli's essays. She seems to be extremely

creative and seems to understand what you are requesting of her. Why is she still getting Ds?"
Kelli brought home a note the next day. It said:

> Dear Mr. Downing:
> The reason Kelli is getting Ds in
> English is because she don't do her
> homework.

That solved the mystery. It was bad enough that the English teacher did not know how to spell Kelli's last name, let alone that she did not know her grammar. How can we expect someone to teach a child proper English when she *don't* know how to speak it herself?

The status of education in America today is further proof that liberal solutions have not worked. They have not aided, as they should have, the minorities, the disadvantaged, and the common folk. When we talk about improving our society, positioning it to realize the great dreams of our Founding Fathers, we are talking first and foremost about education.

To build a decent life for yourself, you must have the proper building materials. But look what has happened to our schools. When I went to school in the forties, the major disciplinary problems were chewing gum, speaking without permission, and not putting wastepaper in the basket. Today, those minor offenses have been replaced by drugs, alcohol, assault, and pregnancy—all the legacy of the liberals who rearranged our society over the past forty years, socially engineering it to make it "better."

Most adults, let alone students, would find such an environment threatening, so it is hardly surprising that teachers pass on their most troublesome students regardless of their competency. The result is 23 million

Americans who cannot read and countless others who do not know how to use the telephone, how to manage a checking account, or how to count their change at the grocery store.

Let's take one hard look at those facts and determine to stop the great educational experiment in America. Forget about new math and new reading methods. Let's go back to the basics of reading, 'riting, and 'rithmetic and at least teach our children how to survive in today's world.

We must start by cleaning up the learning environment, and this is such a natural instinct in our adult world that I cannot understand why it is ignored in school. Let me explain.

Suppose, for example, that you work on a loading dock, in an environment where most of your coworkers are trying to get by. They are basically honest people. Some work harder than others but, for the most part, they do what has to be done and use their pay to attain a measure of comfort and joy.

Then Sam is hired. He has a disconcerting habit of calling the foreman "motherfucker" to his face, but since the foreman, incredibly, puts up with it, you make allowances. Sam obviously comes from a culturally deprived background; you have to be tolerant. Already, by this one simple act of disrespect, Sam has cheapened the environment for you all.

Before long, Sam begins to dominate some of the other workers. He pushes them around, and "borrows" a few dollars here and there after making veiled threats.

The smell of alcohol is often on Sam's breath. Once, the foreman catches him puffing on a marijuana joint and passing it on to another worker. There are rumors that Sam knows where to get "crack."

One day, when a secretary is at the loading dock on an errand, Sam slaps her on the fanny and leers at her. She is enraged, but decides not to make waves by reporting the incident.

Sam takes to boasting about packing a gun. His friends, of the same ilk, start hanging around the loading dock, interfering with everyone's work.

The foreman, having finally reached the limits of his endurance, confronts Sam with all these violations of company policy and human decency, not to mention lawbreaking. Sam responds with a carefully placed punch to the gut, where it will not show.

The foreman, thoroughly intimidated, ponders what to do. He is now afraid to fire Sam, for he knows the madman will try to get even. Instead, he writes a glowing recommendation that results in Sam being promoted to a better job off the loading dock. The foreman has found the solution. He has given over his problem to someone else.

As preposterous as it seems, this is exactly what we do in our school systems. Our schools are populated with honest, hard-working kids who desire to prepare themselves for the challenges of adult life. Yet they are forced to coexist with aspiring criminals who lower the standards for all.

So, first, let's get the troublemakers out of school. Maybe we need a two-tiered system of schools, one for those students who behave themselves and one for those who do not. This second school system for the Sams of the world might be one level removed from reform school. Emphasis there would be placed upon behavior first, and education second. Sure, this might provide a lesser level of educational accomplishment (although Sam is likely to learn precious little in a regular school), but it would achieve two things: It would teach the troublemakers that they must conform to certain standards of behavior, and that, in our world, this is even more important than knowing the three R's. Second, it would clean up the environment in the basic school system and allow teachers to teach and students to learn.

If you would not countenance someone like Sam on the job, why in the world would you send your very own children to schools where Sams roam the hallways?

Why? Because the pabulum-puking liberals want you to believe that Sam, underprivileged and abused by society, deserves a second, third, fourth, and umpteenth chance. Their common solution to one of Sam's frequent offenses might be something like a three-day suspension, which, to Sam, is a three-day vacation. So long as the system lets Sam get away with his antisocial behavior, he will continue to exhibit it.

I refuse to accept the bleeding heart contention, that Sam, at the age of fourteen or fifteen or sixteen, cannot assume a measure of responsibility for his actions. For God's sake get him away from the others before he infects them, too.

Now, once we have cleaned up the environment, let's strengthen it. There are few greater, more unselfish gifts to humanity than the work of a capable, motivated teacher. Let's make sure they are capable, then motivate them.

Anyone who has lived and worked in the world knows that people come in various shapes and sizes, with varying degrees of competency. There are competent and incompetent bricklayers, plumbers, doctors, lawyers, race car drivers, bureaucrats, and presidents, so why should it come as a surprise that there are competent and incompetent teachers?

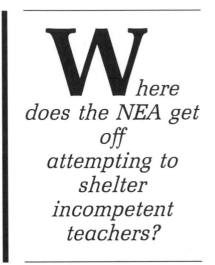**W**here does the NEA get off attempting to shelter incompetent teachers?

For years the National Education Association, which should be called the Teachers' Union, has opposed the administration of competency tests to teachers. This is as crass and short-sighted an example of union featherbedding as there is. If I run the Ajax Aluminum Siding Company and I find that one of my workers installs every other piece of siding upside-down, why should I not be able to fire him for his incompetence? Similarly, where does the NEA get off attempting to shelter incompetent teachers?

On my radio show in Chicago a few years ago, I gave a competency test, right on the air, to a man who had dropped out of the sixth grade twenty years earlier and had never been back to school. He passed it easily. Yet this was the same

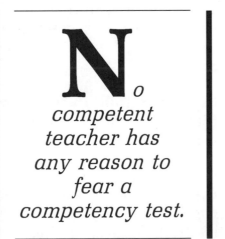**N**o competent teacher has any reason to fear a competency test.

competency test that 15 percent of the teachers in Texas had failed (when they were retrained, only 5 percent of them failed).

This is what the NEA is complaining about? Well, I say, shame on Texas for giving such an easy competency test and shame on the NEA for opposing it. No competent teacher has any reason to fear a competency test.

Once we have weeded out the incompetents and determined that our teachers are capable, we must motivate them properly. Given the sad state of our public schools, it is little wonder that many teachers have lost the dream they once had, the dream of molding young minds and preparing them for life. We must re-motivate the teachers so that they can motivate their students. And we can do this by addressing one issue we have ignored far too long. We give only lip service to our reverence for the teaching profession, and it is about time we put our money where our mouths are. Teachers are *more* valuable to our society, perhaps, than doctors, lawyers, and politicians combined, but with the exception of housewives and mothers, are the most grossly underpaid. It is time to demand that our teachers get better pay. We should, perhaps, double their salaries overnight.

How do we pay for this? First, by cutting down on the number of pabulum-puking administrators who now spend the bulk of their time on disciplinary problems.

Second, by drawing money away from some of the liberals' classic failed solutions, which I collectively call the poverty industry. We reduce as much as possible the amount of money we give away to people for nothing; instead, we give them a better opportunity to learn to earn it for themselves and, in the process, make their own special contribution to the fabric of our society.

If need be, we cut back on the extracurricular activities of school. Sure, extras are important to life. Sports, music, and dancing are all fun, but our schools have come to use these activities as opiates. What good are the extras if you cannot read or write?

If we cannot have it all, if we cannot afford to provide our children with a full range of preparatory experiences, then let us demand that our school system reorder its priorities and accomplish a few simple tasks before it concerns itself with the extras. We should demand that if a school system bestows a diploma upon a student, it is certifying that the graduate can: a) read; b) write; c) perform basic arithmetic.

Is this too much to ask?

If the graduate can accomplish these three tasks with a measure of competence, he will head out into the world possessing the basic abilities to continue to learn for the remainder of his life. If he then chooses to learn geometry or French, if he chooses to read Chaucer or Descartes, if he chooses to play the sousaphone or to play lacrosse, he will have some idea of how and where to begin.

March that graduate from the auditorium stage, diploma in hand, to the public library, show him row upon row of the collected works of human knowledge and wisdom, and say, "Now you can begin to learn!"

Somewhere along the way we lost sight of the fact that education is a preparatory experience. The goal of many high school students is to *get through* and the goal of many teachers is to *get them through.* To hand a diploma to an eighteen-year-old who cannot read, write, add, subtract, multiply, or divide is a crime. But it is the victim who is punished. The incompetent graduate is sentenced to a life of continuing incompetence, because he is thrust into the world lacking the basic tools for survival.

No wonder he is unemployable.

No wonder he goes onto welfare.

No wonder he winds up in jail, for it is the milieu in which he is the most comfortable.

9
Welfare

▷

"WHAT THE HELL IS THIS SHIT DOING IN my room?" I said, unable to hide the anger from my voice. In front of me, on a table in my hotel suite, were four thin rows of white powder, arranged with military precision.

My guest, a man I will call Jerry, was surprised at my vehemence. I was set to host a reception at this plush Chicago hotel. It was a business function to promote my NBC radio show. Jerry, an important businessman from Kentucky, had arrived early, with a beautiful but slightly-used-looking woman on his arm.

The consummate yuppie, Jerry had assumed that everyone at the reception would enjoy snorting cocaine.

"I have that there for the party," he said defensively. "Some of the people might want it."

"I don't like that shit going on in my room."

"You don't have to use it," he concluded with self-righteous logic.

Jerry and his date left to freshen up.

As a law-abiding citizen, I probably should have called the police immediately, but I realized that there would be uncomfortable ramifications. I was known in Chicago for my vigorous opposition to illegal drugs. This was *my* hotel room. The press would love the story.

So I did the next best thing. I took a deep breath and blew the shit off the table, scattering it onto the carpet. Now, only the maid's vacuum cleaner would get high.

Suddenly I had a crazy idea. Caterers had set up a coffee urn in the room. On impulse, I grabbed a couple of packets of Equal, the sugar substitute, tore them open, and arranged the sweet, white powder on the table in four crisp lines. Then, Kim and I went downstairs to join the rest of our guests.

Several minutes later Jerry and his girlfriend appeared, weaving toward us unsteadily. Jerry had a silly grin spread across his face.

"What the hell have you guys been up to?" I asked.

Jerry leaned close and whispered, "We destroyed those four lines. That's the sweetest goddamn coke I ever snorted."

As Jerry tottered off, Kim asked why I was laughing. I told her what I had done. "He's been snorting Equal," I said. "He thinks he's high as a kite."

That is a true story, but it is also a parable. There is both humor and pathos in Jerry's ability to convince himself that he is stoned. Moreover, there is a great lesson here. Jerry is a typically gullible American. He believes what he wants to believe. His mind convinces him to accept a false sense of reality. He wanted to get high, so he did.

In a very real sense we have played the same prank upon a huge portion of the American populace. For years we have allowed them to snort Equal and given them a false sense of security. We have thrown them a placebo and hoped it would make them high. They would be content, and we could forget about them.

The victims are the poor, and the Equal we have allowed them to snort has been welfare.

How could we have fallen for such a scam?

Well, the rhetoric sounded good. There are millions of people in this country whose income is well below the poverty level—or is nothing at all. We cannot let them starve, so we will give them money.

Fine. Life is not fair, and there will always be a portion of the populace that simply cannot work because it is physically, mentally, or emotionally disabled. We must care for them if we wish to call ourselves human. But that group of unfortunates represents only a tiny portion of the Americans who today receive public assistance payments, food stamps, and other forms of welfare. There were not enough of these people, so we *created* an entire subculture of Americans who could qualify for welfare. We gave them Equal to snort so that they would come to believe that they, too, were physically, mentally, or emotionally disabled.

How could we be so cruel? Why did we do it?

We did it so that welfare would become the cornerstone of the poverty industry. Today, some 800,000 jobs depend upon the poverty industry. It is human nature that a bureaucrat is not going to work himself out of a job. To maintain the job positions within the poverty industry, therefore, one has to maintain a clientele. And if your poverty industry is going to grow, you've got to widen the customer base—create more poor people so that you will have more jobs to fill. Somebody has to give them the Equal to snort.

The poverty industry is one of the most insidious

institutions ever to arise in the country, and it will never be abolished until we realize one key fact: *The welfare system does not help the poor, it makes them victims.*

The subject of welfare is not a racial issue—and yet it is. There are more whites on welfare in America than any other race, but that is only because there are far more whites in America. Proportionally, blacks and Hispanics suffer the most

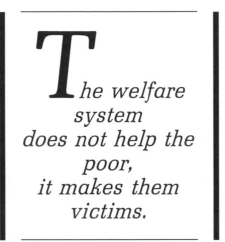

The welfare system does not help the poor, it makes them victims.

from the great socioeconomic, pabulum-puking travesty of welfare. In modern America, it is difficult to separate the subjects of poverty and race.

So let's talk about race.

Racial prejudice has been a problem in America from the moment the white man set foot on the land and began killing Indian "savages." Those same early pioneers and their descendants then systematically turned up their noses at a variety of ethnic groups who immigrated later: Germans, Italians, Slovaks, Poles, Ukrainians, Jews, Irish, ad infinitum. If you could not trace your ethnic ancestry back to Plymouth Rock, you encountered prejudice when you landed in America. The great melting pot did not blend ethnic groups as easily as the history books contend. Often, the pot had to come to a boil before the ingredients became a cohesive broth.

Prejudice takes many forms, but perhaps the most

visible and debilitating is job discrimination. In my father's youth the Boston want ads still carried notices
that proclaimed "Irish need not apply."

How did the various ethnic groups contend with
blind hate?

Here is a story I believe is representative. It was told
to me by a close friend, who asked to be identified only
as Bill.

Bill is a third-generation American. His grandparents
immigrated from the "old country" early in the twentieth century. It happens that they were German, but
they could have been from almost anywhere.

Bill's paternal grandfather did not adjust well to life
in the New World. He took to drowning his problems in
drink, and he died young, leaving three teenage children.

The young man who was to become Bill's father was
an intelligent, capable individual who knew he had
much to offer the world. He was an accomplished
singer, exhibited a definite flair for art, and could pitch
a baseball with authority. But he was left fatherless at
the age of sixteen and had to quit school. Where was
the promise in his life now?

Fortunately there was no welfare system then, no
complex poverty industry, so the young man took the
only viable alternative. He found a job in a factory,
and he turned his talents to use there. He did not like
the work, but he did it to the best of his ability, for
success at the menial job was critical to the new
dream that was forming within him.

He met a girl, a beautiful young woman with talents
and dreams of her own. They courted and married. In
the due course of time they were blessed with four
children, one of whom was Bill.

Throughout his childhood, Bill remained blissfully ignorant that he was 25 percent of his parents' goal. His father still hated his job, but gradually worked himself up higher in the company. He left home at 5:30 every workday morning *for forty years* for the simple, attainable goal of doing his job to the best of his ability. His mother, talented and brilliant enough to have fashioned her own professional career, stayed home to nurture the family.

Only later, when Bill had children of his own, would he be capable of appreciating the enormity of those sacrifices. He gained the first insight to them on the night of his college graduation. Diploma in hand, he hugged his father and was surprised to see tears flowing freely from the "old man's" eyes.

"Why are you crying?" he asked stupidly.

His dad replied, "Every father wants to see his children do better than himself."

And that is how they did it, gang. That is how the Germans, Italians, Slovaks, Poles, Ukrainians, Jews, Irish, and all the other ethnic entities became Americans. They did it in a cross-generational leap. It took one good, decent, hard-working mother and father willing to sublimate their own dreams so that their children might enjoy a better world.

Can blacks and Hispanics do the same thing?

Of course they can, *and they are!*

Enough remains of the American dream to have spurred countless heroic black and Hispanic parents on to the same commitment exhibited by Bill's parents. They scrape for jobs. Somehow they find them, and once they latch onto them they never let go. They work their butts off for the simple, yet all-powerful goal of securing a better future for their children. The greatest worker in America today is a motivated minority, because he or she has more to gain from success and more to lose from failure.

Oh! cry the pabulum-pukers, it's not the same. Blacks had to rise from slavery. Blacks and Hispanics *look* different from white people, so they suffer more from prejudice. They *sound* different. You are talking about a few special individuals with the ability and tenacity to overcome built-in social handicaps. The majority of these people need special assistance.

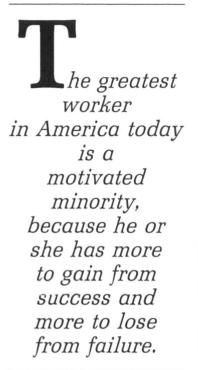

The greatest worker in America today is a motivated minority, because he or she has more to gain from success and more to lose from failure.

We swallowed that line for thirty years. The problem is, it failed, and it failed because it is phony.

Irish immigrants came from a system that virtually enslaved them. Hassidic Jews obviously looked different. Italians, Germans, Poles—all the ethnic groups—sounded different. They all faced special problems.

Certainly the problems faced by blacks and Hispanics were magnified. The civil rights movement of the 1960s, of which I was an integral part, sensitized America to those problems. To the nation's credit, it responded. It legally removed many artificial barriers. But to our everlasting shame we not only allowed the emotional barriers to remain in place, we fortified them. We gave our minorities special considerations which proclaimed in vivid words: We will give you more help *because you are inferior.*

Instead of encouraging them to participate in the American dream, we took it away from them! We gave them Equal to snort, instead of following the simple and obvious course of action—allowing them to *be* equal.

The Equal we gave them is welfare money and the only thing we demanded in return was their dignity.

Is equal such a difficult word to understand?

Two secretaries apply for a job. The white woman can type 85 words per minute and the black woman can type 60 words per minute. Is it equal opportunity to give the job to the black woman? Every day on the job she will know that her performance is inferior, and she will extrapolate that to the belief that *she* is inferior.

Is it equal to hire a black bricklayer rather than a white bricklayer, even though the white man is skilled enough to work 50 percent faster? Every day on the job the black will feel like a charity case.

Is it equal to give someone more money for doing nothing than he could earn by grilling hamburgers at Wendy's? Are we not telling this man or woman, we don't want you to work?

In fact, we are telling them that in so many words. A friend of mine in Cincinnati owns a sandwich shop and he had difficulty keeping workers on the payroll at $5 an hour, until he realized that a woman from the local welfare office ate lunch there, and as she sat at the counter she told his employees they were stupid for working when they could get more money on welfare— and get medical benefits in addition.

We have created an entire subculture that believes it

is stupid to do the one thing that made America great. Work!

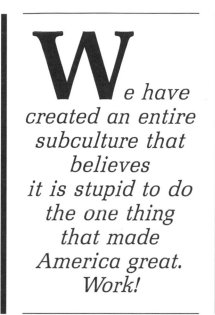

We have created an entire subculture that believes it is stupid to do the one thing that made America great. Work!

Is it any wonder that one all-too-prevalent racial stereotype is that blacks are lazy? They are not. I have worked side by side with too many of them to believe that vicious lie. But I can buy the concept that welfare recipients become lazy because we teach them to be. Indeed, we have paid them to be!

Sometimes we despair that we will ever be able to change the world. We look at all we have done, and it is not enough. There is still so much misery.

Our empathy for the poor and underprivileged is a noble emotion, and one of the special characteristics of Americans. It is just that we have, by and large, gone about it the wrong way.

It was a priest, along with ex-congressman Tommy McGrath, who helped me find answers. I met the priest, strangely, when he was the chaplain of a cruise ship and I was a passenger. His name was Father Tom Rooney. The year was 1967.

During the course of the cruise I befriended Father Rooney, and learned how he had wound up in this unlikely position. He explained that he had been a missionary in Nigeria, attempting to alleviate the sufferings of the Ibo tribesmen, who were being systematically obliterated by Nigerian troops. The government had thrown him out of Nigeria, and he had taken this job as a sort of vacation.

I mentioned casually, "If you're ever in Washington, D.C., and I can help you in any way, give me a call." I wrote down my address.

Three weeks later, at 7 A.M., Father Rooney knocked upon my door, and he lived under my roof for the next four years. From that point forward we directed our efforts toward the organization of what became known as the World Mercy Fund.

We raised $500,000 from USAID and got material help from Pfizer Chemical Company and American Home Products Company. Nurses and doctors and beautiful, ordinary people volunteered their time. Over the course of several years we constructed sixteen of what we called "cottage" hospitals, each with less than fifty beds. Schools, small factories, and roadways sprang up to serve each new community.

And here was the key: Nothing was free. We did not wish to start up a whole new welfare state wherein misery became self-perpetuating. We allowed these Nigerians to maintain their dignity. We allowed them to work for their benefits. If you wanted medical care, you had to bring something—a chicken egg, a yam, a table, a chair, a basket. If you were a poor bush tribesman, you could bring a rat or a monkey.

Ten years later we had created self-sufficient communities. We had cut the infant mortality rate by 67 percent. We had allowed the people themselves to build a new society, wherein they were healthier and happier, and billowing with pride.

Could we do the same thing in Buford, South Carolina or Harlem?

Of course we could.

All we have to do is stop giving out free rides and give back to the honest and talented poor of America what we have for so long denied them: their human dignity.

The *only* way that blacks and Hispanics can merge into the societal mainstream is the way the other ethnic groups have done so, and that is by accepting the necessity of the cross-generational leap. Blacks know that. Hispanics know that. But there is no way that any parent on welfare is going to reach such a goal. The most likely future for the child of a welfare parent is to wind up on welfare himself. The poverty industry is self-perpetuating.

So how do we destroy it?

The simplest way would be to scrap the entire welfare system with one stroke of the President's pen. That, of course, is not feasible, nor would it be humane. Through welfare we have created a subculture of people who really are second-class citizens, and we cannot throw them out into the cold. Their plight is not their fault; it is the fault of the politicians who turned them into second-class citizens by treating them with snobbish contempt disguised as enlightened liberalism.

There must be an interim solution, and here is my four-stage proposal:

Make us all equal; give welfare to every American.

For starters, give every family of four $12,000 a year, and pro-rate that amount depending upon the size of the family. This money comes with no ifs, ands, or buts. No taxes. No constraints. You do not lose the money if you go out and get a job. If you drink the money away, gamble it away, or spend it on women, that's your tough luck, buddy. It is the extent of your free ride.

The second tier is this. You can earn another $12,000 tax free. That means you can take a job at $6 an hour, add that income to your $12,000 of welfare, and pocket the entire amount. You can have $24,000 a year to participate in the American dream, and pay no taxes.

The third tier really begins to separate the worker bees from the drones. There will always be a segment of society, whether white, black, yellow, red, or purple, who will be content to remain in the first or second tier. If you want something more, you have to work hard for it. Every penny of your annual income between $24,000 and $48,000 will be taxed at a 50 percent rate. If you earn $48,000, you will pay $12,000 in taxes —returning to the government its welfare payment.

In the fourth tier, the sky is the limit. Everything you earn above $48,000 is taxed at a flat rate, such as 28 percent or 35 percent, high enough to provide the necessary funds to run the government.

This simple plan is dependent upon one other, equally simple plan, detailed in the next chapter.

It could work, gang. It could restore dignity to human labor. It could restore pride to millions of Americans whom we have suppressed for decades.

The only problem is, it would put the 800,000 bureaucrats who currently run America's poverty industry out of work . . . but let them go out and compete in the free marketplace.

10

Taxes

THIS WILL BE A SHORT CHAPTER, BECAUSE
the subject is absurdly simple.

Perhaps the biggest political joke of the past few
years was what was called "tax reform." What it accomplished is this:

- Some people paid less tax.
- Some people paid more tax.
- Everyone was confused.

Am I off base in thinking that "tax reform" and "tax
simplification" should have been the same thing? Congress reformed taxes in much the same manner as a
janitor who sweeps the dust from one room into the
other. It simply rearranged the dirt. The current mishmash of tax laws, before and after reform, is *the* greatest proof that we do not have representative government, for the common men and women of America—
almost as one—grow livid at the mention of taxes.

Every responsible American recognizes the need to

support government. No one really wants to part with the money, but we all know that there is a price for democracy. What galls the average American about taxes however, are two simple words: unfairness and waste.

We are not talking here about classic forms of government waste such as absurd cost-overruns on military contracts or welfare abuse. Let us here speak only of the tax money that is wasted by the tax system itself.

One fallout of tax reform was the necessity to employ an army of Internal Revenue Service employees to man the Tele-Tax Information Service to answer questions about the new tax law. Never mind the fact that these "experts" gave out the *wrong* information 20 percent of the time. Even when they were to be believed, they were still earning government salaries paid for by our tax dollars.

This is only the tip of the iceberg. Consider the multitude of IRS employees who must sift through millions of complex returns searching for errors, oversights, and evidence of fraud. Consider the cost of creating and printing volumes of complex tax forms, instructions, and explanatory bulletins.

Go outside the government and you will find that H&R Block has made a fortune because our government insists upon propounding confusion. And H&R Block only gets the relatively simple returns. Private accountants handle millions of intricate returns that cost the taxpayer dearly.

Why is this so? Just look at your 1987 Form 1040 package of Federal Income Tax Forms and Instructions. A letter on the front from Lawrence B. Gibbs, Commissioner of Internal Revenue, states: "Our goal is to MAKE TAXES LESS TAXING . . ." This absurd statement is followed by two copies of Form 1040 (which alone asks for sixty-five different entries), six tax schedules (in duplicate), five further sets of forms (also in duplicate) with individual instructions, and fifty pages of general instructions! Of particular interest is the information on page 49 which tells you how to order more forms and instructions. In modern America death is far more certain than filling out an IRS form . . . and may be preferable.

Could anything be more patently absurd?

America's income tax system is downright stupid. This is not the fault of the IRS. It is ludicrous for one and only one reason: because Congress, over the years, continues to pile on one exemption, deduction, regulation, and demand after another in order to serve the desires of special interests.

America's income-tax system is downright stupid.

We countenance this fiasco only because the IRS has done a superb job of making us fearful of the consequences. Take one look at that confusing package of tax information—realize that you can go to jail if you fill it out improperly—and you run screaming to a tax accountant for help.

Thus we have an entire industry, both within and without government, that makes its living in nonproductive, nonessential labor.

On the surface this is wasteful, and beneath the surface it is cruelly unfair. The more money you have, the more likely you are to employ an accountant—or a firm of them—who can steer you toward the greatest loopholes. You can be sure that, as long as the tax law remains as complex and incomprehensible as it is, the common man and woman are the ones paying more than their fair share.

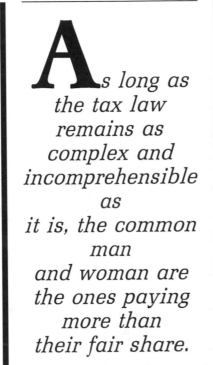

As long as the tax law remains as complex and incomprehensible as it is, the common man and woman are the ones paying more than their fair share.

There really is only one solution. We all know it but our politicians refuse to act.

I am not generally in favor of book burning, but I will make an exception in this case. Start a huge bonfire on the steps of the Capitol, haul out volume after volume of the tax code, and throw them onto the pyre!

There is a key concept to true democracy: There are no special interests. Nowhere is this basic law of human decency flaunted more than in the tax code. Do away with it! For God's sake, scrap it!

Let simplicity reign. Let the number of exemptions, deductions, and special exemptions for individuals and businesses be this: Zero.

Require everyone to pay the same percentage of tax on the same level of income, with no ifs, ands, or buts.

The result will be that we will all pay less, for our taxes will no longer fund the public and private bureaucracy that sucks our blood.

Sharp accountants are all in favor of the idea. They can turn their skills to basic matters of business efficiency. As for the less talented accountants, not to mention the IRS's Tele-Tax Information experts, let them pursue a more productive line of work, such as building shelters for the homeless, growing food for Ethiopians, or burning marijuana fields.

One final note is of paramount importance. If we can get it through the special-interest-thickened-skulls of our legislators to scrap all tax deductions, we must hold them by the hand and continue to remind them:

Leave it alone.

11

Crime and
Punishment

I̶ₙ 1957 I RECORDED A SONG ENTITLED
"Boulevard of Broken Dreams," written by Harry War-
ren and Al Dubin. I had no idea how prophetic that
title was.

The record began to take off, and a promotional tour
was arranged. I received a $5,000 advance against roy-
alties, deposited the check in my account, and left Los
Angeles for a whirlwind tour that included the most
profitable vehicles for popularizing a new record, Dick
Clark's *American Bandstand* show in Philadelphia and
his Saturday night show in New York City.

By now I had been away from my father for years,
and something within me longed for reconciliation. After the show, I called Hyannisport. "Hiya, Pop," I said.
"Did you see me on the Dick Clark show?"

My father replied, "You were the biggest embarrass-
ment I've ever had. You can't sing. You're off key. Nobody liked the song."

Once more I was banged by my dad, and astounded by the depth of his anger. He was retired now from the performer's life I was only beginning to live—and he could not tolerate any hint of my success in his field. He still wanted me to be a lawyer or a businessman—anything but a performer.

I was determined to rise above this unfathomable vehemence. I remained on the road, doing the shows, plugging the song, paying my travel expenses by writing checks on my account back in L.A.

When the tour ended and I was back on the West Coast, it took me a few days to settle down. Finally I dived into the stack of mail that had piled up and came upon a bank notice informing me that the $5,000 check I had deposited prior to my tour had been returned because of insufficient funds. Naturally this had snowballed. Other letters from the bank were in the mail also, containing several of my own checks that had bounced. I was overdrawn by $203.

I was on my way out of the apartment building to go cover the checks, when someone called out behind my back, "Hey, Mort!"

I turned to see a man I did not recognize. "Are you Morton Downey, Jr.?" he asked.

Assuming that he was one of my new body of fans, I replied, "You got it, pal," whereupon he slapped handcuffs onto my wrists and hauled me off to the Hollywood lockup.

This was crazy. Why were they arresting me for $203 worth of overdrawn checks that were clearly not my mistake?

My manager posted $50 in bail to get me out and my father, hearing of this new trouble through my brother Kevin, hired a lawyer for me.

The case dragged on for some time. I viewed it as a minor offense that did not concern me greatly. Finally my day in court arrived and my lawyer convinced me to follow a simple strategy. I would plead guilty—because I, indeed, had written checks with insufficient funds—but I would plead *guilty with an explanation.* This allowed me to detail for the judge the extenuating circumstances. The only reason the checks had bounced was because I had been paid with a bad check myself. And the reason I had not taken care of it immediately was that I had been out of town, on a promotional tour.

The judge said, "Ninety days in the county jail!"

I could not believe my ears. They were sending me to jail for a "crime" everyone commits by accident once in a while? True, I had some "bouncers" in my day, but this was the pits.

Only years later would I learn that my father's hand was in this jail sentence. Through his many contacts in California, and particularly through his good friend, Pat Brown, who was yet to become the Golden State governor, my father had arranged to teach me a lesson. Many years later I would be able to prove that and have the conviction overturned.

> **I** *could not believe my ears. They were sending me to jail for a "crime" everyone commits by accident once in a while?*

But at this moment I faced the next three months of my life in the slammer.

For the first three weeks I was kept in the Los Angeles County jail, thrown in side by side with every manner of lowlife imaginable, and some pretty nice guys, too. At this entry level of the criminal justice system there is considerable mixing of the populace. Here are convicted drunk drivers and vagrants forced to consort with murderers, rapists, and thieves awaiting trial.

My short-term strategy was to avoid the heavy-duty criminals as much as possible and to prove myself a model prisoner. I donated blood. I kept my mouth shut and my ass covered.

Since I was serving such a light sentence I was soon transferred to a minimum security farm. Here, too, were a surprising number of hardened criminals. I adopted a stronger strategy now by joining the prison boxing team. Every Friday night I got my brains beat out in the boxing ring, but during the rest of the week I was left alone by the prison breed of semi-humans who prey only upon the weak.

After sixty-one days in hell, having earned time off for good behavior, I was released.

I was bitter, but I was wiser. I had learned two unforgettable lessons.

The first was that I never wanted to go back again. Ever.

The second was that I was lucky to have spent relatively little time there, or I might well have gone back. My brief experience was enough to show me the absurdity of the American prison system. We have long made a fundamental mistake concerning our prisoners, and it is costing us dearly.

This is hardly a unique observation on my part, and it is so obvious that I cannot quite understand why we allow the situation to persist. If you throw five good apples into a vat of garbage, when you pull out those apples, they will be covered with garbage. The same is true of jail. Why, with all our supposed sociological enlightenment, do we continue to throw a handful of minor offenders—those convicted of victimless crimes, such as prostitution, simple drug possession and gambling—in with the scum of the earth? Thirty years after my own experience, I still cannot answer the question.

Until we develop a two-tiered corrections system, crime will continue to plague us, for we allow the hardened criminal to infect the young and relatively innocent, making them rotten also.

We've got to make it easier on the low-level criminals, and tougher on the vermin.

We've got to make it easier on the low-level criminals, and tougher on the vermin.

As it is today, prison is not such a bad place for the career criminal; in some ways, in fact, it may be better than the outside world. He does not have to worry about paying the rent. He knows where his next meal is coming from. He does not worry about providing for his family; the welfare state will take care of that. His friends are handy. He has television. Drugs, alcohol, and sex are available. And each and every day the courts send him a batch of fresh meat, new victims whom he can terrorize, rape, beat, extort, and murder. A considerable portion of the prison populace never had it so good on the streets.

We allow this ridiculous state of affairs because we continue to hearken to pabulum-puking sociologists and psychiatrists who continue to make excuses for the scum of life. There are deep, hidden reasons for violent crime, they tell us. Society (you and I) is at fault for the emotional trauma we have inflicted—or so they would have us believe. This may be the greatest extant example of cruel and unusual punishment inflicted upon our collective spirit.

Sure, social conditions have played a role in all of our lives. But the bleeding heart collection of Freudian windbags has somehow sold us (and particularly our judges) on the patently ridiculous concept that there can be any excuse whatsoever for brutality, rape, and murder. Thus, we pay lip service to the concept of re-habilitation. We call it "corrections." We somehow buy the notion that the murderer should have a second chance, even though the victim cannot possibly have the same opportunity.

What does a second chance produce? It produces a 67 percent rate of recidivism (and those are the ones who are caught). The *great* majority of criminals, once released, take up where they left off, without even a whimper of remorse.

I remain confident that this is going to change. It is too stupid. Deep inside, any relatively law-abiding citizen knows that we have allowed our prison system to become a joke.

We *must* do two things.

First, anyone convicted of a "victimless" crime, a misdemeanor, or a minor felony—on their first offense —should not be sent to jail or prison. These are the only lawbreakers who do, statistically, stand a good chance of being "corrected." Make their punishment hurt, but keep them out of prison. Give them severe and extended community service tasks to perform. Let them rehabilitate rotting apartment complexes to house the homeless. Instead of removing them from society, let them help society, and at the same time care for their families so that their families do not become wards of the welfare state, thus making society a twice-burned victim.

Second, concerning the hardened criminal, we must say to the bleeding-heart Mr. Sociologist, "Zip it. Sit down and shut up."

My father's father was brought up in a slum and he did not become a hardened criminal. Go back a generation or two and you will find societal factors rampant in your family tree that could have borne rotten fruit. So why aren't you a thief, rapist, and murderer?

Let's stop making excuses for crime and start handing out appropriate punishment.

Let's overthrow this notion that there is good in everyone. Some people are just plain evil and no amount of counseling and rehabilitation is going to change them.

Let's overthrow this notion that there is good in everyone.

Life is not fair. It never has been and never will be. But it would be a lot less dangerous if we kept the rotten apples in their own stinking barrel.

Let's change metaphors. If your dog had rabies, would you lock it into a pen with healthy animals? Of course not. It is not his fault that he has rabies, but is that reason enough to spare him? Of course not. You may love that dog deeply. You may berate yourself for not having him vaccinated. You may shed tears over his fate. But in no way, shape, or manner will you allow him to infect any other form of life. You will not allow him to plead guilty to the lesser disease of distemper in return for a lightened sentence. You will not give him time off for good behavior. You will lock him into a cage and throw away the key.

Or you will destroy him.

Which brings us to a related topic.

I have friends on the police force in Cook County, Illinois, who tell me that during the twenty-year period when the state had a death penalty law, only two policemen were killed in Chicago. In the twenty years since the Supreme Court voided Illinois' death penalty, twenty-six policemen have been murdered.

Tell me, Mr. Pabulum-Puking Liberal, that the death penalty does not deter murder.

Tell me, Mr. Pabulum-Puking Liberal, that the death penalty does not deter murder.

Most slayings are not first-degree murders. They arise from domestic arguments and are often committed by people who have never before been in trouble with the law. For these regrettable but heinous crimes, we need a life imprisonment sentence that means what it says, not one that carries an assumption of parole in a decade or so. There may have been extenuating circumstances, but these count little to the victim. Let the common murderer pay for his crime by remaining in prison for the rest of his life. Forget about rehabilitation. Perhaps he can serve society best as a bad example.

But there are other forms of murder that cry out for stronger vengeance: cop killing, the killing of a prison guard, mass murder, brutal murder, murders committed during the commission of another crime. We need to send a strong message to the rabid animals who would commit such crimes, and it is not that they will be freed to walk the streets in ten years or so. Let them walk the streets of hell. We need to demand payment in kind.

Until we do that, we will continue to see the erosion of respect for law and order. By our lenience we have allowed our criminal element to declare open season on law enforcement officials. And if we allow the situation to continue to deteriorate, we will see the growing phenomenon of the vigilante society.

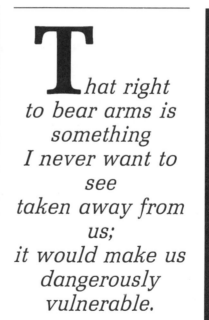

That right to bear arms is something I never want to see taken away from us; it would make us dangerously vulnerable.

This is one strong reason why there is so much sentiment in the nation to preserve the American right to bear arms. The Constitution says we have that right, but there are those who would like to take it away from us at the very time we need it most. Some even contend that what the Constitution really guarantees is the right for the militia to bear arms, and to them I say, study your history. At the time the Constitution was written, the militia was the people. There was no draft, no organized army. Everyone was a member of the people's militia. That right to bear arms is something I never want to see taken away from us; it would make us dangerously vulnerable.

At the same time, why cannot we approach the issue with a bit of common sense? The right to bear arms certainly does not mean the right to carry a nuclear weapon in your hip pocket, so it must have limitations. Should not one of those limitations be dumdum bullets that expand when they hit the target and are known by the blatant nickname of "cop killers"?

I believe that the gun lobby, the National Rifle Association, is way off base when it argues against restricting weapons and ammunition. It is afraid that if it gives ground on one issue, it might have to give up on all of its aims. We need some basic political compromise here. Handguns, yes. Rifles, yes. Uzi submachine guns and dumdum bullets, no.

Let's retain the ability to protect ourselves, while making it tougher for the criminal to attack. Because—make no mistake about it—as the years pass, if we see no improvement in our criminal justice system, we will be more inclined to use those guns.

Suppose your daughter was raped and murdered. What caring father, knowing the current state of the criminal justice system, knowing that the criminal will probably be released in ten or fifteen years—or less—would not get down on his hands and knees and, with tears streaming from his eyes, pray, "Dear God, let me catch that bastard before the police!"?

I would. And if I caught him, I would become the

judge and the jury, with no compunctions about it whatsoever. No matter how much I might fear going back to jail, I would consider that, in this one instance, two wrongs would make a right.

I am not proud of that sentiment, but I think that every decent person nowadays feels a little bit of vigilantism, because he realizes that our law enforcement agencies have their hands tied.

And perhaps this proves my earlier point about the prison population. We allow the rabid animals back out onto the street. Perhaps they are beginning to infect us all.

12

Religion

THERE'S A SONG I SING EVERY MORNING, AS
I prepare for the day:

Good morning, dear Jesus, I love you,
Good morning, my heavenly Pal.
I hope the world is what we want it to be,
Everyone can live in peace and harmony.
Good morning, dear Jesus, I love you,
Good morning, my heavenly Pal.

My wife, Kim, once said to me, "Isn't it disrespectful
to call Jesus your pal?"

Of course not. He is my Pal. He has given me everything I have ever asked for, and piled on top of that
every test that I have required to make me strong
enough to exhibit His love to the world.

Oh! I can hear my critics cackle. They paint me as

vitriolic and hateful and sick. They cannot conceive of me being motivated by love.

This is because they are not paying attention. I love Jesus. I love Kim. I love my daughters. I love my late father. I love the human spirit. And I love my critics, too. Study carefully the suggestions I am making in these pages and you will see that they are all motivated by deep love.

That is what religion is all about.

To me, religion is intensely personal. It may be my loudmouth style to rant and rave about the evils of the world (as a matter of fact, Moses, Jesus, and Mohammed were loudmouths, too), but I tend to keep my religion to myself. For the record, I am a practicing Roman Catholic. I believe that God is the Father Almighty and that Jesus is His Son. I believe in the Holy Spirit, working quietly to nurture humanity. I believe in heaven, and I believe that too many people live out their hell right here on earth. I believe in right and wrong, good and evil, as clear and identifiable concepts.

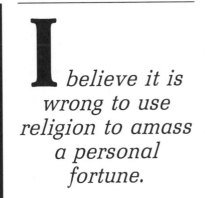

I *believe it is wrong to use religion to amass a personal fortune.*

For example, I believe it is wrong to use religion to amass a personal fortune. Jim and Tammy Faye Bakker, Oral Roberts, Jimmy Swaggart, and others of their kind sicken me. Nowhere in my Bible do I read that religion will make you rich. Rather, I read, ". . . it is easier for a camel to go through the eye of a needle, than for a rich man to enter into the kingdom of God."

As of this writing, the Bakkers and Jimmy Swaggart have both fallen from grace, ostensibly repented, and appear poised for comeback attempts, with or without the endorsement of their respective churches. My Pal Jesus has some advice for them: "If you would be perfect, go, sell what you possess and give to the poor, and you will have treasure in heaven . . ."

I suspect, however, that these rich preachers would respond to that advice in the same manner as the Judean yuppie whom Jesus addressed directly. The man ". . . went away sorrowful: for he had great possessions."

The "Pearly Gate" scandals of recent times also bring to mind an Old Testament quotation, uttered by King David: "How are the mighty fallen!"

All of this has been very good for religion. The moneychangers have been taking over the temple and we should have cleared them out long ago, so that we can get back to true worship, which is simple communion with God.

I am not alone in this belief. Stop people on the street. The great majority will tell you that they believe in God, and that He is a source of great comfort to them. This is clearly a majority viewpoint in America, and always has been. The human spirit knows intuitively that a higher authority rules our shabby lives.

Yet our leaders exhibit a strange, ambivalent attitude. We have prayers to open congressional sessions and prayers to inaugurate the President. We have an invocation at the Super Bowl, for heaven's sake. Why, then, can we not have prayer in schools?

No one says you have to force a student to pray to Jesus, Jehovah, Allah, Buddha, or the spirit of his great-great-grandmother, but cannot he be allowed to take a moment at the beginning of the school day to commune with a greater power?

The Supreme Court says no, which must be confusing to students who stand up to recite in unison the Pledge of Allegiance, which clearly states that this nation is "under God."

Then they trudge off to history class to study the Declaration of Independence, which asserts that "all men are created equal, that they are endowed by their Creator with certain unalienable Rights . . ." They read further and learn that the brave men who declared our independence did so by "appealing to the Supreme Judge of the world" and "with a firm reliance on the protection of Divine Providence."

They must be thoroughly confused by the time they get to the First Amendment to the Constitution, which declares, "Congress shall make no law respecting an establishment of religion, or prohibiting the free exercise thereof . . ." That is clear to me. There shall be no official religion, thank God, but neither shall there be any impediments to the practice of religion.

The Founding Fathers of this country did not all belong to the same church. They were not even all Christians. But they shared a deep conviction—and put it in writing—that the nation's survival depended upon the will of God.

Well, gang, it still does.

13

The Homeless

SLEEPING ON A PARK BENCH IS NOT TERRIBLY uncomfortable if you have the good fortune to become impoverished in California, as did I. After my father used his influence to block my career in show business, and had me thrown into jail as an educational experience, I bummed around for several years, trying to make a go of it as a rock 'n' roll singer. When I could I found work as a short-order cook, laboring all night so that my days were free for writing, singing, rehearsing, and auditioning. I picked up $15 apiece for singing on "demo" records—recording new songs for writers so that they could then attempt to peddle them to record companies. Perhaps the best demo I recorded was a song entitled "Splish Splash." Using my demo, the songwriter persuaded a major label to produce the record, and to let him sing the song himself. His name was Bobby Darin.

Jobs came and went. I poured what money I had into my music, leaving me little to live on.

My preference in living quarters was the bus station, but if it was too crowded, I would find a park bench, usually in the vicinity of Grauman's Chinese Theatre. I learned to sleep sitting up, so that I would not be rousted by a policeman or rolled by a mugger.

As a young man, temporarily down on his luck but confident of ultimate success, I could withstand a year or two of such indignity, but my heart goes out to those who are sentenced to a life on the streets, particularly a New York City street in bitter winter. In addition to their physical danger and discomfort, I grieve for their battered spirits. These are people who have been defeated by our system. Society has told them they have no valuable contribution to make. Frustration as much as poverty drives them onto the park bench.

Tʜe widening gap between rich and poor in America is forcing more and more of these people onto the streets.

I am not talking here about the individual who makes a competent and intelligent choice to be homeless. There is a romantic element to genuine hoboism that will always be with us. Nor am I talking about the infirm, the deformed, and the mentally incompetent. I accept it as a given that we should be taking care of these unfortunates and it is a blot upon our souls that we do not.

But let us address the issue of the new and growing

breed of homeless, the erstwhile middle-class men and women without money, jobs, loving families, and homes. The widening gap between rich and poor in America is forcing more and more of these people onto the streets. How can we countenance this?

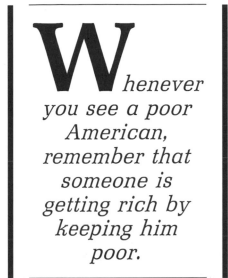

Whenever you see a poor American, remember that someone is getting rich by keeping him poor.

We do so only because the homeless are an important part of our poverty industry. If we did not have the homeless, how could we pay the owner of a welfare hotel $3,000 a month to provide shelter? Whenever you see a poor American, remember that someone is getting rich by keeping him poor. This is such a simple truth that even an economist could figure it out. Government statistics show that we spend about $21,000 of our tax money on each poor person per year, yet the actual benefits they receive amount to only about $8,000. Where is the missing $13,000? In the pockets of the 800,000 bureaucrats who administer the welfare industry. Management, mismanagement, waste, and theft eat up most of the money.

Look at how the situation developed in New York City, and how it is growing worse every day. The great metropolis is caught in a strange housing bind. There is only a 2 percent vacancy rate in apartments. It is very difficult to find an apartment in New York. Yet at the same time there are 78,000 apartment units standing vacant because they have been condemned. Over the years, as the city steadily raised property taxes, landlords found their margins of profitability squeezed by taxes and rent control. They let the property fall into disrepair. They could not or did not pay the taxes, allowed the government to foreclose, and presented New York City with a glut of dilapidated buildings unfit for human habitation. The South Bronx today is one huge pile of rubble, reminiscent of Cologne, Germany, after World War II.

Instead of paying $3,000 a month to a welfare-hotel owner, why not loan *the $3,000 to the family itself and turn the able-bodied homeless into urban homesteaders?*

While these buildings continue to rot, the city houses as many homeless families as possible in rattrap hotels and pays the owners as much as $3,000 per month for the rooms. Many of these buildings are little better than the condemned apartment units. The plumbing is bad. The heating is bad. The air-conditioning is nonexistent. They are dens of drug sales. People disappear into these holes forever.

Somehow we are supposed to feel like good people for doing all this for the homeless.

Now let us make a wild assumption that a portion of these unfortunate victims of our poverty industry are willing to better their lot. Why do we not give them the opportunity? Instead of paying $3,000 a month to a welfare hotel owner, why not *lend* the $3,000 to the family itself and turn the able-bodied homeless into urban homesteaders? The government has played a large role in the decay of those 78,000 condemned units, so why should it not pay to turn the situation around?

This is not an original solution. I have borrowed elements from the late Senator Bobby Kennedy and from Senator George McGovern. They enunciated the beginnings of a workable plan.

Sure, many of the homeless are already too beaten to take advantage of the opportunity, but others are not. Our welfare mentality continues to assume that handouts are the solution to poverty, ignoring the obvious truth that productive work is the solution to poverty, and ignoring the equally obvious truth that hordes of good men and women are willing to prove it.

So I say to the politicians, read my lips:

. . . there are 78,000 vacant, condemned apartment units in New York;

. . . there are thousands of men and women down on their luck, out of work, out of hope;

. . . you are paying someone else as much as $3,000 a month to house them.

Can't you figure out a solution?

14
Labor

THROUGH THE GRACE OF GOD AND EQUAL
doses of luck and hard work, I was finally able to build
an economic future for myself. In the sixties and early
seventies, bowing to my father's wishes, I established
a successful business career, first working in management for the Canteen Corporation, the large vending
machine company, and later starting my own Washington, D.C., consulting firm, Government Legislative Con-
sultants, lobbying for several major U.S. companies.

I had left show business, but I could not stop writing
songs. Frustration poured out of me in the words to
"From L.A. Baby":

Everyone's a big producer
With Oscars in the can.
In a dingy back room on the top floor
Is where you'll meet the man.
He'll let you star in his home movies,

He'll take you to the top.
Then he'll toss you to the bottom of the heap
So fast you just won't stop.
And people with the right connections
Will really plug you in.
Come back home from L.A., Baby.
Leave the films to Rin Tin Tin.

Up until now I had always had to scrape for the rent money; finally I had some cash to play with. Fulfilling a long-held fantasy, I marched into an auto dealership and paid $6,700 for a brand-new 1967 Lincoln.

I brought it back the next morning. It had the worst damn rattle I had ever heard in a car. Weeks went by as the mechanics tinkered. They tried everything. We could tell that the irritating noise came from the vicinity of the left rear passenger door, but no one could find an obvious problem. Finally, in desperation, mechanics used blow torches to cut out the quarter panel. Inside they found a tuna can with a bolt in it. The can had been welded into place. This was no accident. Someone wanted that car to rattle.

Through the car's serial number, Ford investigators traced the car back to the assembly line and identified the culprit, a disgruntled employee who resented anyone who could afford to buy a Lincoln.

Is it any wonder that Japanese cars took over the market?

What happened to America's work ethic? This was a nation that prided itself on its work, that would take on any nation product-for-product. We were blessed with a mother lode of raw materials and a workforce—the sons and daughters of pioneers—second to none.

Our achievements did not come without struggle. Tension is a natural state between a boss and his employees, and America experienced its share. As the nation industrialized it passed through a period of laissez-faire, a fancy French word that allowed management to get away with about anything it wanted.

The labor union movement countered. In an epic struggle that spanned decades, brave union organizers suffered and died so that workers might have their natural rights. They succeeded beyond belief. There is no national holiday called Management Day.

Thus we achieved equilibrium, a balance between the rights of management and labor, working together toward a clear goal: outproduce the rest of the world. The height of our industrial triumph occurred during World War II. We did outperform the rest of the world and we won the war as a result.

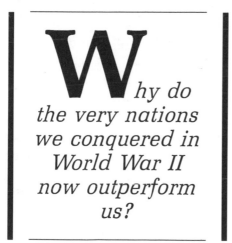
Why do the very nations we conquered in World War II now outperform us?

Why, then, some forty years later, do the very nations we conquered now outperform us?

For one important answer, let us look at the typical work day of a man we will call John L. Hardnails, president of one of America's most powerful labor unions. He arises at 7:30 and scans the *Wall Street Journal* as he sips the morning coffee brought to him by his maid. He showers, shaves, dresses in a tailor-made suit and silk tie, and climbs into the back of his chauffeured limousine. On the way into the city he places an early call, via carphone, to his stockbroker. He arrives at the office in time to be briefed by his aides prior to a 10 A.M. press conference. A board meeting follows, then an extended, leisurely, three-drink lunch with his West Coast vice president. He dictates some correspondence in the afternoon, but he leaves early, for he and his wife have complimentary theater tickets for the evening. It will be a late night, which is tough on him, for he has an early flight to Miami the next day.

Do you see? It has been years since this man represented labor, if he ever did. He is *management!* He is masquerading as labor.

Suppose his union goes on strike. Do you think he will give up his maid for the duration?

Union leadership has abdicated its responsibility to represent its people. Rather, it represents neither management nor labor, but its own dubious existence. One of its primary foci of attention is its Political Action Committee, whose first and foremost job is not to influence politics, but to preserve and protect the cushiony positions occupied by the union leaders.

It is time for the workers to regain control.

If unions were abolished overnight, I have no doubt that we would quickly return to the abuses of laissez-faire. I don't want them to go, but they must be turned around. Just as we have allowed misrepresentative leaders to take control of our government, so, too, have we allowed men like the not-so-mythical John L. Hardnails to take over the unions. They have continued to paint management as the enemy long after management has been conquered, so that you would continue to support any union activity, no matter how absurd.

And I mean *absurd.* Some examples:

- The Teamsters' Union, long the epitome of corrupted, nonrepresentative, *criminal* leadership, is today the union of tens of thousands of American *policemen*! How could policemen vote to join the Teamsters' Union?

- A steel mill in Pennsylvania was going broke and proved it by filing for bankruptcy. It announced that it was going out of business unless union workers agreed to take a pay cut from $25 an hour to $16.88 an hour. In response, the workers went on strike, brandishing placards that proclaimed: We Won't Work for Slave Wages! Well, gang, if there ain't no money, there ain't no money. None of the striking workers seemed to be able to understand that management's offer amounted to $16.88 per hour *more* than the alternative.

- This is supposedly a nation of free speech, right? Why is it, then, that I must pay dues to the American Federation of Television and Radio Artists/Screen Actors' Guild—or I will not be allowed to utter a single word on the air? My right to free speech costs me approximately $8,500 per year.

Unions are big business now, and they should be subject to the same restraints that we put on big business, but no one has yet exhibited enough guts to do that. Suppose that an investigation revealed that Lee Iacocca had skimmed millions from the Chrysler Corporation pension fund. He would be thrown into jail and perhaps joined by his entire board of directors. Workers would sue. The public would boycott the product. Chrysler would go bankrupt and the public would say, "It serves them right." But few people seemed to care that the Teamsters' Union systematically gutted its pension fund. Now they represent our police.

There is another glaring example of how we allow unions to operate with impunity, which becomes more apparent when we apply it to management. Suppose that the state of New Jersey passed a law declaring that all of its residents had to buy their gasoline from Exxon—or forfeit their driver's licenses. That is absurd, of course, and no one would stand for it. Yet state after state has passed laws forcing you to join a particular union if you wish to hold a particular job.

Whatever happened to free enterprise? Sell me on the virtues of your union, don't force it on me. Prove to me that by joining I will receive greater pension benefits, a better health-care plan, and a stronger voice in job-related concerns. But don't force me to pay the dues, because then you have no incentive to give me value for my money. No wonder unions, and their leaders, have grown fat, dumb, and happy. In today's society it is a paradox that the man who is supposed to represent labor may have the softest job.

Unions should and must have every right to organize. But they have no right to coerce anyone to join them.

America's labor unions should be one of the greatest powers for social good. But we have,

No wonder unions, and their leaders, have grown fat, dumb, and happy.

in our apathy, allowed them to fall into the hands of selfish managers. We exhibit the same lackadaisical attitude toward union elections as we do toward political elections. We rubber-stamp the ballot, and we deserve the kind of leadership we get.

We get leadership in the United Auto Workers that kicked and screamed against robotization. The leaders seized on this issue and used it to keep attention focused on the "enemy"—management. And it proved to be a good short-term strategy. No one wanted to lose his job to a robot. This was typical of the type of issue that dominated labor unions over the past two or three decades. The leaders remained blind to the fact that change is a way of life. Instead of helping their members adjust to change, they fought it. Thus they contributed to a major alteration in global economics. The Japanese robotized, and convinced millions of Americans that they could build a better car. The proof is in the sales figures. If American and Japanese cars offered a relatively equal value for the money, very few Japanese cars would be sold in America.

God bless them, they did it. The Japanese benefited from the fact that we had bombed out all of their factories and felt so guilty about it that we gave them billions of dollars so they could start from scratch. But that alone was not enough. They latched onto emerging technologies, managed to robotize *and* give their workers lifelong job security—and they beat the pants off of us.

What did the antiautomation stance of the American labor unions give us? Short-term job security and a long-term pain in the butt. If the union leaders could envision that it might take four workers to maintain the robot that took over four assembly line jobs and assemble 25 percent more cars, they did not say so.

Part and parcel of the problem is that unions have undermined—and dangerously so—the value of work. They have forced management to pay more for less. In the short-term this is to the benefit of the fortunate few, but over a period of time it destroys our incentive to do good work. If your job is secure from competition and you get paid the same whether you assemble 12 or 73 widgets per hour, why bother working hard?

As I write these words, I have in my hand a ballot from my union, AFTRA/SAG. Broadcasting executives want to cut back on some of the residual fees paid for certain types of announcements and commercials. The union is mad about this and has called for a strike.

I am one who is likely to earn less money if the union loses the battle, but I will vote no on the strike authorization. I think I am already overpaid for what I do, and this prevents other talented people from being able to get into this industry. The big bucks can only go to a few.

When I signed the contract to host my television show, I could have pocketed more than $1 million up front. But why should I do that? What if the show had been a flop? Why should I rip off $1 million? Instead, I agreed to take much less in salary in exchange for a percentage of ownership in the show. That does not make me a gambler; it makes me an American.

Look at the four possible outcomes and you will see what I mean:

Let's say I took the $1 million. At the end of the one-year contract the show is canceled because of low ratings. The station has taken a bath. I am out of a job, but I have the after-tax residue of $1 million in my pocket. Am I happy? Of course not. I am a rich failure.

Suppose the show is a hit. My agent now settles into a combative posture with management. "Phil wants $30 million a year!" he screams. "Oprah wants $30 million a year! Mort should get $30 million a year!" We finally settle upon some exorbitant figure after estab-

lishing ourselves, for all time, as management's enemy.
And we have further escalated the prices we all must
pay for entertainment. Now I am part of the reason it
costs $40 for a seat to a Broadway play, or $25 for a
basketball ticket.

But I did not take the $1 million. Suppose the show
flops. I am unhappy, perhaps depressed for a time. But
I am an able-bodied American worker. I can take care
of myself and my family. I can pick myself up and start
over again without an additional burden of guilt for
having ripped off the station.

What has, in fact, happened, is that we have a hit
show on our hands. Thanks to the collective efforts of
my entire staff, we have persuaded 15 million people to
watch us every night. Now, in fact, my share of ownership is worth far more than the $1 million I turned
down, but management does not begrudge me that, for
they appreciate my willingness to wager on my own
abilities. When my agent sits down with them to nego-
tiate a new contract, he is not placed into an us versus
them situation because us *is* them. I am a part owner of
this enterprise. I am both worker and management.

Incentives such as these need to be structured into
every job. The American worker is smart enough to
know that he should get paid, not because he is an
American, but because he is a *worker.* He is fed up
with a union boss who tells him that the guy next to
him deserves the same pay for less work.

The 1987 strike by the National Football League
Players Association was an example of how labor relations are beginning to change. Regardless of one's sym-
pathies, there was a key lesson for the American
worker, and it is this: Management, despite the power
of unions, has learned that you are not indispensable.

Owners waved good-bye to the union players and

brought in new players in their stead. If you were pro-management, you called them replacement players. If you were pro-union, you called them scabs. Regardless of the term, you could not escape the reality that, with each passing Sunday, more and more fans were accepting them as the real thing.

Abuses occurred on both sides. Management is no better or worse than labor. But when the smoke cleared, more than eighty of those replacement players had proven themselves capable enough to stick around. All they needed was a chance.

Union members be forewarned: Produce good work for management, or it will find others who will. Management has suddenly remembered that America is a free market. No matter how secure your union leaders try to make you feel, be assured that there are plenty of "replacement players" out there ready and willing to take your job. The featherbedding days are gone.

I am one worker convinced that you can't fool all of the citizens all of the time. I believe that the American worker is developing a renewed sense of commitment to his job. I see some encouraging signs of change. I see people, common folk on the assembly lines and behind the deli counter and on the construction site, who are returning their attention to the essence of the workaday world. They have remembered a secret that our ancestors knew when they came here to build America: Do the best job you can do and you will be rewarded. They have accepted the fact that life is not fair. It does not parcel out the same abilities and opportunities to us all. But they know that if they do their jobs, whatever they are, to the best of their abilities, no one is going to be able to prevent them from making money. Sure, they can organize into a common labor force and lobby for improvements and a greater slice of the pie. But those efforts mean *nothing* unless they are working as hard as they can. They realize that the only way to get this nation's economy back on its feet is to build a better car than Datsun, Nissan, Honda, Mercedes, and BMW.

We can do it. We did it before. All the other nations of the world marveled, and scrambled to catch up to us. Now we have to catch up to some of them. Are we afraid of that challenge?

Of course not.

15

Feminists

IN 1978 GLORIA STEINEM CHARACTERIZED ME as the most dangerous male reared in the twentieth century. It is difficult for me to imagine a greater compliment, considering the source. She made that statement in a fund-raising letter for Senator Bob Packwood (R–OR), who was running for reelection. I was campaigning against him because he was in favor of legalized abortion.

What I particularly liked about Steinem's comment was that I knew it would make me popular with women. Already, by 1979, the signs were evident that the Steinems, Abzugs, Friedans, and Smeals did not represent the interests of the majority of American women. Radical feminism is dead. Hallelujah!

Perhaps the greatest evidence of that came during the 1984 presidential election. During his first term, President Reagan maintained his strong opposition to the Equal Rights Amendment, the issue that Steinem and her sisters had championed. The feminist leaders would have you believe that they spoke for the downtrodden American woman, but, in 1984, the American woman stood up and spoke for herself. Women cast the majority of votes in the 1984 election, and more than 60 percent of those women voted for President Reagan. It was the American woman who reelected an anti-ERA president.

What she said to her self-professed leaders by means of that vote was: "You don't represent me. I have two children. I am raising them at home and holding down a job, to boot. My primary responsibility is those children and I will do the best job I possibly can. And you are not going to make me feel guilty, Miss National Organization of Women, because I prefer motherhood as my career. So zip it. Hear *me* roar!"

The primary mistake of the feminist leaders was their assumption that their voices emanating from New York and California were representative of women in North Carolina and South Dakota when, in fact, the great media centers are the two areas of the country most out of touch with the mainstream. Insulated in the ivory towers of their metropolian milieus, the feminists failed to perceive that, had they structured their message properly, they might easily have accumulated a majority in favor of their cause.

They failed to understand that the issue never was women's rights. The issue was, is, and forever will be, human rights.

As it happens, God created humans in two basic forms, and most of us thank Him daily for His brilliant planning. The feminists erred in discounting the deep appreciation women and men have for differences in body, mind, and spirit.

Sure, there were grievances that needed to be ad-

dressed, for both sexes. What fair-minded individual could be opposed to an issue as basic as equal pay for equal work? Who could argue that a career-minded woman should not have society's blessing to compete and achieve in a world artificially dominated by men? Who could argue against the need for adequate day-care facilities for the children of women who chose to —or had to—hold down jobs outside the home?

But social movements tend to carry issues to excess, partly to drive home their basic points, and feminism was no exception. Mainstream Americans came to differ with the feminists on a few relatively minor, low-priority issues: Why should a woman sports reporter be allowed into a male locker room? Did we really need a girl on the high school football team? Women really began to note the absurdity of the Equal Rights Amendment when they realized it might cause their daughters to be drafted.

There is no question that the feminists struck some raw nerves. Women suffer the effects of discrimination in America; so do men. Women are not quite sure how to deal with it; men are equally unsure. But women are no longer willing to listen to the rhetoric of the self-styled feminist leaders; and neither are men.

Those spokeswomen simply could not understand the reality of the average American woman, who did not live in a New York or California apartment, participate in consciousness-raising sessions with the sisterhood, or sit in a circle on the floor to develop a war strategy. The average American woman was not concerned with the issues of the political world, but about the greatest of all worldwide issues: How can I best nurture my family? She might catch some of what Gloria Steinem said to Phil Donahue, but her attention was likely to be distracted by a dirty diaper or a skinned knee.

Early on, the American woman did hear enough of the feminist message to be thrown into turmoil. What was she doing at home wiping snotty noses when she should be out directing corporate mergers? The rhetoric was strong enough to persuade numerous women to take a shot at long-festering careers.

So what happened? Millions of women attempted to switch their priorities, looking suddenly outward instead of inward. They marched into the workforce with a vengeance. For some, it turned out beautifully. Capable men did not fear their competition; in fact, they welcomed and applauded the achievements of equally capable women. (Incompetent men were threatened, but who cares?) The majority of women soon realized, however, that they had achieved a hollow victory. The feminists had made them feel guilty about staying home. Now their hearts made them feel guilty about forsaking the home.

The feminists countered with an absolutely stupid strategy. We began to see the veneration of the "superwoman," the female who could do it all, manage a fast-rising career (this was always mentioned first) *and* nurture her family. Here was a message applicable to perhaps one-tenth of 1 percent of the women *and* men in the country, and it brought the feminist leaders further away from reality.

Only now have some of them begun to acknowledge that motherhood is, perhaps, a noble, fulfilling career all its own. But it is too late for the feminists, who have by now exposed themselves as total phonies who never grasped the fundamental truth that, while women had and have many legitimate gripes, they had no desire to change their basic orientation as women.

Give the American woman and man their choice of life-styles, and I contend that the majority will opt for the roles I described in twin songs:

A Woman Has to Know

A woman has to know
That she's needed all the time,
When her troubles grow too heavy
There's a smile.
See his slippers lying there
By his favorite easy chair
And the comfort in just knowing
All the while
That when six o'clock is near
She can take him in her arms
And feel his strength
Go rushing to her soul.
All the trouble of her day
Slowly rises,
Fades away
When a woman
Has her man
In her arms.

A Man Has to Know

A man has to know that he's needed all
The time, for the little things he feels
He can do.
If the kids are feeling ill, good ol' dad
Will pay the bill. If his Christmas gift
Is charged, he'll pay that too.
And when six o'clock is near he can
Hold her in his arms and feel her strength
Go rushing to his soul. All the troubles

Of his day slowly rise and fade away,
When a man has his woman in his arms.

The great *strategic* mistake of feminism was to ignore the fact that women and men thrive in their traditional roles. Whether by heredity or environment, the
sexes are far more different than feminists wished to
acknowledge.

The great *tactical* mistake of feminism then compounded the error. Having ignored the ingrained orientation of women, the sisterhood chose to embrace the
one issue they could never win. Joining in league with
the medical establishment, feminists directed their major effort to a campaign worthy of Adolf Hitler. They
discerned that the major obstruction to a woman's career was the "unfortunate" and recurring phenomenon
of birth. Babies were holding women back; therefore,
we had to do away with them. Feminists actually had
the audacity to assume that the American woman
would support their campaign to allow mothers the in-
discriminate right to murder their unborn children.
They ignored the one strongest passion in the female
breast—the passion of motherhood. This was one of
the most flagrant political miscalculations of all time,
and the feminists are now seeing the results in ever-
dwindling support.

Thanks to their zealous advocacy of the so-called
right to abortion on demand, the pabulum-puking feminist leaders have lost their following, and I can say to
Gloria Steinem, "You are, thank God, not the most dangerous female reared in the twentieth century."

16
Perversion

W<small>HEN</small> I <small>WAS ELEVEN YEARS OLD, OUR</small>
family doctor examined my genitalia to ascertain
whether I was developing normally. He spent an inor-
dinate amount of time on the examination, eventually
placing my young penis into his mouth.

This was strange and frightening medicine indeed. I
knew something was despicable about this man and
his actions, but I was naive and afraid to confront authority. At the time, during my parents' bitter divorce
battle, I was living with my grandmother and she
seemed ancient and unapproachable. So I told no one.

As the years passed and I learned more about the
world, I realized that this doctor was a pervert, a ho-
mosexual pedophile. For a long time I assumed that *all*
doctors were of the same ilk. Did they teach that in
medical school?

My wife, Kim, was also sexually abused when she
was six years old, by a friend's father.

As far as I am concerned, hatred for sexual perversion is one of the noblest passions within the human breast.

The above information should give the shrinks all the ammunition they need to analyze and explain my consuming hatred for sexual perversion. Fine. As far as I am concerned, hatred for sexual perversion is one of the noblest passions within the human breast.

Look around these days, and you find more and more of it to hate. The more I talk about it, the more I find people who have been victimized by it, and their stories don't just involve dirty old men, but also fathers and mothers and teachers and trusted friends.

Perversion is particularly appalling when the victims are children. Are there more cases of sexual abuse in children today than in previous years? I don't know. Perhaps it is merely being reported more openly and realistically, and that is good. But what bothers me is that our government seems to be taking an ever more active role in dealing with it, and I wonder whether the bureaucracy has intruded too far in determining how we raise our families.

For example, when I was a child, the government saw nothing wrong with a father who administered a good thrashing once in a while; today, the existence of a few blood blisters on your child's behind could send you to jail. Not too many years ago any social worker would argue that when a child reports sexual abuse, it *must* be true, because children do not make up such tales. That may have been true in the past, but we now have evidence of cases where pabulum-puking psychiatrists have manipulated the testimony of innocent children (in effect, abusing them mentally and emotionally) to build cases of sexual abuse that were not really supported by the evidence.

This is a tough call. Certainly abuse should not be tolerated, but neither should we tolerate unwarranted intrusion. I wish I had better answers on how to define and prove child abuse, but I do know this much: We should proceed with caution.

And I do see a disconcerting trend to make the victims of child sexual abuse wards of the state. Look what this does. First, some scumball of an adult family member destroys the child's emotional and physical equilibrium. Then, the state takes the child away and thereby destroys what is left.

For God's sake, let us keep these poor victims out of the hands of the state, and the only way to do this requires a farsighted and unselfish sense of commitment. Let the state say, "Aunt Mary, or Uncle John, can you care for this child? Can you raise him, nurture him, love him, better than his parents and better than the state?" We must do our best to keep these children within the bosom of the family—if not with the parents, then with the closest loving and capable relative.

Love is the operative word here. The state can provide food, shelter, and clothing. But it can never provide love. And without that love, the child is likely to grow up to be a carbon copy of the abuser, another sexually disoriented adult in search of fresh victims. At the very least, he or she will find it difficult to establish an ongoing, loving relationship with another adult.

And we need this so badly! While I wish no suffering

or disease on anyone, the recent rise in the occurrence of social diseases has at least served to bring to an end the sexual revolution, as well as to the frantic game of singles bars and musical beds that is the antithesis of love.

Listen to these words from a thrice-married man who lived enough of his life single to have seen the hollowness of promiscuity, and who now realizes that the best definition of safe sex is sex with someone you love and to whom you are deeply and irrevocably committed. Listen to these words from someone who believes that it is "macho" to say: "Only you, Kim, now and forever."

My church and the Surgeon General of the United States will tell you that abstinence is the best protection against social disease; I tell you that love is.

If love controls your passion, you will not do anything that might put your lover at risk.

In today's world, the further one moves away from the beauty and holiness of an act of love between husband and wife, the more one exposes his or her body and soul to danger, an issue I spoke to in a song entitled "Moth and the Flame":

When you play the game of love
The wheels spin round and round,
The stakes are high,
You bet your heart on love
But sometimes the loser will cry.
Our moment burns bright,
Then
Good-bye, love.
That's life,
Who's to say
Who's to blame?

If a moth meets his fate at the candle
Is it the fault of the flame?

Look at how people are hovering around the flame today. How can you say you love someone and then commit an act of possible murder by screwing him or her in the ass? I see no evidence of love in that. Love is not getting your rocks off; it is doing everything you can to nurture and protect someone you care for. Love often means denying yourself immediate pleasure for the greater good of the person you love.

Perhaps the greatest love a person can exhibit today is to deny his body to his lover.

I believe that the primary purpose of man is to love mankind. There are, however, certain forms of sexual intercourse—anal, for example—which, given what we are learning about the spread of diseases in general and AIDS in particular, are so wrongheaded and unnatural that they should be outlawed. Such an opinion, of course, flies in the face of the "socioengineers" who have been enlightening our society for decades and who would have you believe that any form of sex between consenting adults is natural and acceptable.

I say, screw 'em—figuratively speaking—for that is just what they have been doing to us. Pabulum-puking may be the most pernicious of all social diseases. Do you suppose the pabulum-pukers have ever scientifically examined the physical trauma which can result from even consenting anal intercourse?

By all means, let us extend this concept to both sexes, lest I be accused of being a homophobe. I am an anal sex-ophobe, and let the shrinks make of that what they will. Anal intercourse is a perversion of life's most beautiful act. It is wrong, just as it is wrong to have sex

with animals, young children, various inanimate objects, and nonconsenting adults.

If today's sexually crazed aberrant does not love strongly enough to look upon his penis as a potential murder weapon, let us then love him enough to force him into abstinence.

I hear the liberals screaming: "You can't legislate the bedroom!"

Who says we can't? We can legislate our society in any way, shape, or form that we wish to. Our elected leaders have a moral obligation to protect the weak of society, the same as a parent has an obligation to protect the interests of the child.

And listen, Mr. Legislator, our children have been misbehaving in the bedroom. You have an obligation to protect them from their own stupidity, foolhardiness, and perversion.

God did not fashion the vagina to accept the American Express card.

Paying for sex is certainly a perversion, too. God did not fashion the vagina to accept the American Express card. Given my druthers, I would wipe prostitution off the face of the earth, but we have ample evidence that this is not going to happen. Even preachers succumb. So, although it goes against my upbringing as a Roman Catholic, I think the time has come to legalize prostitution for the greater good of the human race. This pragmatic compromise has now been made necessary by the onslaught of the

AIDS virus. We cannot continue to allow prostitutes, in effect, to sell AIDS on the street. Prostitutes must be licensed so that they can be tested, and to license them, we must legalize them.

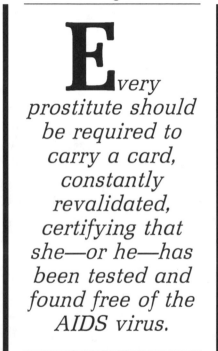

Every prostitute should be required to carry a card, constantly revalidated, certifying that she—or he—has been tested and found free of the AIDS virus.

Every prostitute should be required to carry a card, constantly revalidated, certifying that she— or he—has been tested and found free of the AIDS virus. The simple act of prostitution would no longer be a misdemeanor, so long as this procedure was followed.

But to ply the trade without a valid license should be a *felony,* punishable by a long prison term. As AIDS continues to make inroads into heterosexual society, a prostitute's vagina becomes a deadly weapon, and ought to be considered as such.

It takes two to tangle, of course, so the patron of a prostitute should also be tested and licensed. Decriminalized prostitution could move indoors and attain an air of semi-respectability, whereas street prostitutes and their customers would be punished severely. No longer can we allow the unbridled passions for sex and money to threaten human existence.

This is not a perfect solution, but it is a start.

As far as other forms of sexual perversion are con-

cerned, including homosexuality, pedophilia, necro-
philia—whatever "philia" you care to name—it is obvious to me that they are all crimes, although we have
been conditioned not to call them that openly. But the
perpetrators are not common criminals. They are,
themselves, victims of their own bodies.

We must cease meting out cruel and unusual punishment to them, which is to say, let's stop turning them
over to psychiatrists. We are simply giving one animal
to another. Rather, let us give them a meaningful
chance to eliminate their perverted sexual urges so
that they can contribute to society.

I think the day is coming when Americans will have
had their fill of the abuses of Gay Rights and will rise
up and say, "Yes, we love you, but not your perverted
acts. We want to help you, but you must help your-
selves as well. Think of what you are doing and use a
little common sense. What we are talking about is not
just something 'unnatural,' it is downright dangerous—
especially in these troubled times. Restrain yourself, or
society will do it for you."

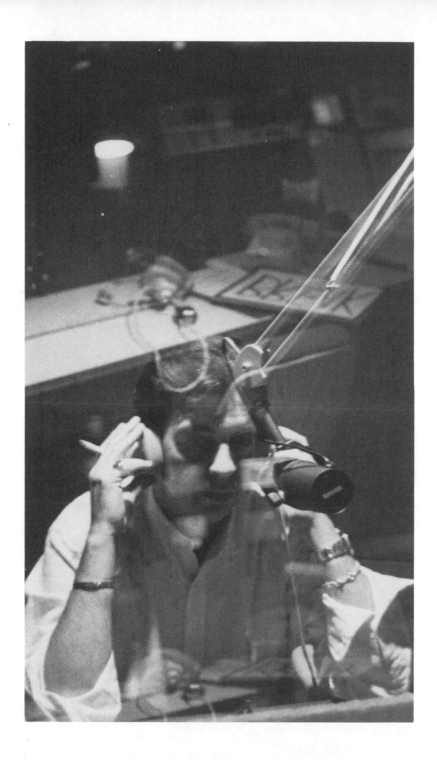

17
The Media

$\triangleright$

Here is a bit of literary criticism, drawn from my old edition of *Encyclopedia Britannica*. It is a thumbnail review of one of the most widely read authors of the past two millennia:

"The Gospel is written in rough, colloquial, sometimes ungrammatical Greek, highly Semitic in coloring —the kind of Greek which might be the work of a bilingual teacher whose native speech was Semitic, and who lacked literary culture."

No wonder St. Mark never won the Nobel Prize.

Our subject matter is less noble than the life of Christ, but those of us who work in and around the media today had better realize that every word we write or utter will be subject to criticism. No doubt St. Mark's words will survive ours, but we must treat our statements reverently anyway, for we live in an age when the ability to communicate has expanded almost beyond belief. Words today reach into every corner of our society, and their impact upon our lives has made the old child's rhyme obsolete. Words *can* hurt, even more so than sticks and stones. They are weapons that today's media wield without mercy.

A case in point:

It was a big day for me. The year was 1959. I had a tryout for a part in an upcoming film to be called *Blue Denim*. I knew it would not be much of a film, but it would give me a foothold. I had already made a bit of a splash in the recording industry, but my path had been blocked several times by my dad. As far as he was concerned, there was room for only one star in the family. But here was another chance to prove to myself —and to my father—that I had the talent to make it on my own.

Shortly after the interview began, the casting agent asked, "Are you honest?"

"Yes, I think so," I replied.

"Do you always tell the truth?"

"Yeah. Why?"

He dropped a newspaper clipping in front of me and commanded, "Read this."

It was Walter Winchell's column from the *Los Angeles Examiner*, reporting that his good friend Morton Downey had informed him that there was a person going around Hollywood calling himself Morton Downey, Jr., saying he was the son of Morton Downey, and he hoped that these people would be alerted that *he had no son by that name*.

I could not believe that my own father would deny me or that Walter Winchell, who had attended my sixteenth birthday party at the Stork Club, would be a partner to such a vicious and obvious lie.

"That's bullcrap," I said to the casting agent. "It's a lie. Here's my driver's license."

The man looked at me with contempt and said, "Anyone can get a driver's license. Save the bull for someone else." As I walked out of the office, he added, "You might have the talent, but you don't have the character to be in Hollywood."

I headed straight for the offices of the *Examiner,* found the appropriate editor, and demanded a retraction.

"We have no control over that," he said. "It comes out of New York. You'd better call Winchell."

"He won't listen to me," I said. "He's a friend of my father." I explained that my father had systematically sabotaged my career, and I could see that he was beginning to believe me.

"Can you prove that you're Morton Downey, Jr.?" he asked.

I had an idea. "Do you have a morgue here, a file of old articles?" I asked.

I dug into old issues of the *Examiner* from the days following my birth on December 9, 1932. Sure enough, in the December 11th issue I found a picture of Morton Downey and Barbara Bennett, holding a little baby. Me. The caption read: "Welcome, Little Stranger. Famed tenor Morton Downey and actress wife Barbara Bennett welcome their first born, Morton Downey, Jr." The brief story reported that the proud father had composed a song for the little fellow, entitled *Welcome, Little Stranger.*

The next day the *Examiner* ran a tiny black correction box beneath Winchell's column, admitting the error.

That did little to endear me to my father, and neither did it get me any work. People tended to remember Winchell's column, not the correction. Those who did see the correction did not wish to get into the midst of a family squabble. All the doors of Hollywood were closed to me.

Years later, when Pierre Salinger was running for the Senate in California, I worked in the campaign. Winchell, whose career had been faltering, was assigned to cover the campaign, and we renewed an old friendship. I let a couple of weeks pass before I confronted him. I said, "Walter, what ever made you write years ago that Morton Downey had no son by the name of Morton Downey, Jr.?"

First, he claimed not to remember the column, then he denied that *he* had written it, saying that maybe one of his "people" had written it.

"It had your name on it," I pointed out. "Didn't you know what went into your column?"

"Not always."

"Then you were intellectually dishonest," I charged. "You had your name on it and did not know what was being said."

Finally he became contrite. He said, "The only thing I can imagine is that your dad and I were such good friends and hung around the Stork Club together, so I might have felt sorry for him . . . and I may have done it as a favor."

I accepted that explanation and let it go at the time. But I thought about it more and more as I entered the world of broadcasting. We have a tremendous responsibility to report news fairly and responsibly. We are the Matthews, Marks, Lukes, and Johns of our day, and if those saints can be attacked for some of their writings two thousand years ago, imagine how we ordinary mortals will be attacked two thousand years from now.

Part of the problem is that the press confuses its self-definitions. Reporters must report all the facts and only the facts. I am not a reporter. Rather, I am one of a growing number of advocates in the media. The difference between me and some others is that I make no pretense of being a reporter. As it happens, I believe that issues are aired more fairly on my show than on the evening news. Everyone gets a chance to speak. My audience may hoot and howl, but only after a person gets a chance to present a viewpoint. There are "bouncers" in my studio to preserve the right of free speech.

Part of that right includes the freedom to criticize, and here is where I take my role as an advocate seriously. I generally have a strong position on any issue and I am not afraid to state it. On the contrary, certain network anchormen and reporters also have strong positions, but they often insert those views insidiously, by a tone of voice, an upraised eyebrow, or by slanting the content of the news. They often cross the bounds of reporting and advocacy without telling you they are doing so.

The press has, thus far, failed to grapple with a basic problem. They are fond of proclaiming their *right* to free speech, yet loath to acknowledge the *responsibility* that goes with it. Freedom of the press is basic to our unique experiment in democracy, but so is the responsibility to police oneself. The *right* to say just about anything must be subjugated to the *responsibility* to be fair, compassionate, and decent.

There is a further issue.

The framers of our Constitution could not conceive of the modern world. When they wrote the First Amendment, they did not have pictures in mind. They did not envision photographs, shiny, chic magazines, motion pictures, and television. If they had seen modern pornography, they would have no trouble recognizing it as such. The would have no difficulty stating that freedom of the press does not include the right to show a picture of a woman sucking a man's penis or pictures of men beating women and putting clothes clips on their breasts. I am convinced that they would argue that some sense of responsibility goes along with the gift of freedom of the press.

The Supreme Court has consistently refused to critically define the bounds of obscenity. In their legal wisdom they have decreed that obscenity is a transient concept continually redefined by contemporary community standards. This gets them conveniently off the hook and ignores the obvious truth that the sleazier elements of the community will chip away at the standards and have you believe that the framers of the Constitution really intended for you to have free access to magazines and videos depicting all manner of human sexual aberration.

Al Goldstein is one of the champions of free sexual expression. He publishes a magazine entitled *Screw* and endlessly cites his First Amendment right to take the media to the farthest reaches of morality. His magazine will routinely show a penis entering a vagina or any other convenient orifice. To me, this and other forms of pornography are the greatest misuse of our greatest freedom. Must we be free to degrade men and women, lower the moral standards of our country, and diminish our value as human beings?

Of course not. The Supreme Court will not acknowledge the fact that if we refuse to define obscenity, others will continue to lower the definition for us. As soon as we accept one specific as the norm, the pornographers find something right next to it that is not quite the norm. They move on to that until we accept the

new norm, and so on, until the contemporary community standard is that there is no standard.

Well, I know obscenity when I see it, so I'll move in where the Supreme Court fears to tread. Let's start with the word *penetration.* Do we have to show one human being entering another? Put that question up for a national referendum and see what Americans think. The answer will be a resounding *No!*

We grew up on violence, as presented to us by Walt Disney and his successors, Hanna-Barbera. The lesson was that violence did not hurt.

Add to that the word *sadism,* and here we enter a realm where our contemporary community standards have been undermined to the point where our sensibilities are now almost deadened. We grew up on violence, as presented to us by Walt Disney and his successors, Hanna-Barbera. The lesson was that violence did not hurt. Wile E. Coyote could blow himself to smithereens and arise intact to continue his quest for a lunch date with the Road Runner. Elmer Fudd and Bugs Bunny have combined to depict some of the most graphic violence ever shown to humanity—without ever shedding a drop of blood. Need we even mention the Three Stooges?

That was all fantasy, of course. The depiction of actual violence probably traces back to World War II, the first time we saw horror pictures of actual life and death. We saw Auschwitz and Buchenwald. We saw human mass graves, stuffed with bones. We began to be desensitized toward man's inhumanity to man. If you look at something often enough, it seems to become normal.

Later we were treated to graphic coverage of the Vietnam war. Every night the press seemed to show ever more horrible and shocking pictures.

Today we will look at almost anything. The press will show us films of people jumping off of buildings, of accident victims being stuffed into body bags. An enterprising reporter will pound upon the door of a victim's home and record the family's most private moments of grief and pain. Film at eleven.

Sadistic is the operative word here, and when you add that element to the portrayal of violence you have taken it out of the realm of normality. You have begun to treat it as a normal human emotion, when it is not normal.

Where do we draw the line on violence? Perhaps we have to look at the motives. If sadistic violence is portrayed as a means of selling a magazine or a movie ticket or of achieving higher television ratings it is without justification. But there can be honorable motives.

This is a tough question, and one that I have grappled with on my television show. I was criticized severely for airing a photograph of a murder victim, a fifteen-year-old girl who had been raped repeatedly before she was killed. The photograph showed her lying upon her stomach with a two-foot wooden stake protruding from her anus.

My critics howled that the photograph overstepped

the bounds of decorum. The great champion of free speech, the American Civil Liberties Union, called it "garbage journalism." But they failed to examine my motives.

First of all, I did not identify the victim or her family. I never showed her face. I never revealed her name. We protected her privacy.

My motive was simple. I had, on the show, a typical, pabulum-puking liberal who was attempting to excuse the murderers because of some Freudian hogwash concerning their childhood trauma and the deleterious effects of societal influences. The most effective way to counter his high-flown prose was to show my audience what these "poor, misguided" youths had done, which was to rape and murder a fifteen-year-old girl and shove a two-foot stake up her anus. There was no way to describe that indignity adequately in words. I used the freedom of the press to show that the murderers were not merely errant youths but degraded animals who committed a crime so heinous that it left no room for forgiveness. I showed the picture to shock the sensibilities of people who look at crime in this country and excuse it because it is committed by "disadvantaged" kids. We have all known plenty of kids from disadvantaged families who did not find it necessary to commit sadistic murder. Who invaded the girl's privacy, me or them?

There really is a very simple way to sort out all the confusion as to the proper balance between the rights and responsibilities of the press. Why don't we take the issue to the one element of society whose speech is most ignored: the common American citizens?

Why not have a national referendum on what Al Goldstein can or cannot publish in *Screw,* what photographs Morton Downey can show, and whether or not

Dan Rather has a constitutional right to sass the Vice
President on the nightly news?

Ask the people.

They will tell you what is obscene and what isn't.

18

Alcohol and Tobacco

WHO AM I TO TALK ABOUT THE EVILS OF smoking?

Second to the Loudmouth, the cigarette is my most well-known trademark. In the development stage of my television show, I made a key decision. I would smoke on the air because I smoke off the air. Constantly.

This makes me unique among broadcasters, who tend to be a smoky bunch but are loath to admit it in public. Peter Jennings would never dream of puffing on a cigarette while anchoring the evening news, but the camera has returned unexpectedly early from a break to catch him in the act.

Not wishing to be a hypocrite, I determined that people would see the real Morton, warts and all. Morton is not an angel. Morton smokes. (Morton also has a drink once in a while and has been known to utter a curse word now and then.)

I have caught some flack for smoking on the air. Jonathan Weiss, representing the American Civil Liberties Union, stood at one of my Loudmouth podiums and said that, although he passionately agreed with me (a shocking admission) on my opposition to euthanasia, I was committing an act of suicide by smoking cigarettes and compounding the felony by doing so on camera and thereby setting a horrible example for my generally youthful audience.

How could I argue? Of course he was right. I have never recommended smoking to anyone. I do not recommend it to my Uncle George, who still smokes two packs a day at the age of 93, nor did I recommend it to my grandfather, who died at the age of 101 with a Philip Morris in his hand, nor did I recommend it to my father, who died at the age of 86 with a cigar in his hand.

Sure, cigarettes may kill me. The only possible justification for my habit is addiction, and I hate the thought of being a slave to anything. The only example I set is a bad one.

I*t is a measure of my addiction [to cigarettes] that I have gotten myself down to only three packs a day.*

So, on the air one night, I announced that I was going to attempt to quit. To my surprise, the audience began yelling, "No, no, no!" and threw cigarettes onto the set. They wanted the original Mort.

Okay. I love my audience. They are the best audience in television, but that does not mean that they are always right. If I can help it, I will not kill myself merely to please my audience.

Sorry, gang, but I am trying to quit. It is a measure of my addiction that I have gotten myself *down* to only three packs a day.

So, who am I to talk about the evils of smoking?

A victim, that's who.

Alcohol and nicotine are drugs just as surely as marijuana, hashish, cocaine, and heroin. But society must deal differently with them, because long ago society chose to allow their use. I do not advocate returning to the days of prohibition, but I do believe that we have allowed the use of these drugs to get out of control, and we need to apply some common sense.

First of all, if we are going to have legal drinking in America, let's keep it that way. I was shocked to learn from a close source that bootlegging is a thriving—and growing—American industry. As much as 28 percent of the alcohol consumed in America is illegal and that means untaxed. This is not confined to the hills of Tennessee, but is rampant in our big cities. Buy a drink in a New York bar and you stand a good chance of consuming moonshine, bought for a fraction of its face value and simply transferred into an expensive bottle. Bootleg vodka is in vogue now, because moonshiners have learned that there is no difference in taste between the cheap and expensive brands. Any perceived difference is merely an advertiser's triumph.

The same is true of tobacco. Trucks loaded with bootleg cigarettes ply the interstates, defying the law, avoiding the payment of state taxes.

This, of course, is a direct raid upon our wallets. Society pays a heavy cost in the annual toll from alcohol and tobacco abuse, and these so-called sin taxes are meant to offset it. When moonshiners and cigarette smugglers rob the government of the tax, they rob us all.

But the patterns of alcohol and tobacco use in this country give us genuine reason for optimism. Here are two areas where we have made some progress, and we should take note of them. They may teach us some strategies to apply in other areas.

It only took one indefatigable mother, grieving over the death of her daughter at the hands of a drunk driver, to alter the nation's attitude toward drinking and driving. Candy Lightner started Mothers Against Drunk Driving and proved that Americans were MADD enough to force the pabulum back down the throats of those who would excuse despicable crime. Our courts are moving toward what should have been the obvious realization that the drunk driver deserves no more special treatment than the man who walks down the street brandishing a loaded gun. Both are carrying a deadly weapon. If one of them kills you, does it matter how?

Similarly, the nation has received the message that cigarette smoking is hazardous to your health. Each year more and more Americans manage to quit. Whether this is merely the result of more health-consciousness, I do not know, but the reduced incidence of smoking does coincide with the appearance of the Surgeon General's warning on the sides of cigarette packs, and with the disappearance of cigarette advertising from television.

Why not extend these proven ideas? Let's put a warning on bottles and cans of alcoholic beverages, noting that more than two ounces of this beverage at any time can create dizziness, disorientation, loss of memory, and, eventually, death. That would be as valid on a bottle as the current warnings on the sides of cigarette packs.

If we truly wish to get serious, we should ban beer and wine advertising on TV. If we cannot advertise cigarettes, why in the world should we be allowed to advertise beer and wine? We could gradually extend that to a ban on all forms of advertising for alcohol and tobacco, including radio, magazines, newspapers, billboards, and even matchbooks. If partial bans have reduced the consumption of tobacco in America, a complete advertising ban on both substances could not hurt, and would quite likely save millions of American lives, not to mention a goodly portion of the estimated $60 billion these two killers cost our economy annually.

We do not have to take the extreme view and ban the substances. But, for God's sake, do we have to promote them?

19

Defense

$\triangleright$

IF YOU LIVE ON ELM STREET AND YOU BECOME aware that a rash of assaults and burglaries is occurring two blocks away on Oak Street, do you ignore the situation? Of course not. You take every means of defense you can against the thugs who have invaded your neighborhood. You bolster the security of your own home and, if need be, you help organize a neighborhood watch to patrol the area.

The world is our neighborhood today, and we must do our part to protect it, otherwise the invasion will eventually move from Oak Street to Elm Street. Fighting an aggressor elsewhere in the world is enlightened self-interest. We are, in large part, doing it for our own benefit.

But is it more than that? Should we be the policemen of the world?

Damn right.

The world is populated by billions of people who

watch with a combination of awe and jealousy as the American dream unfolds. More than anything else they would like to see their own nations offer them the same opportunities for life, liberty, and the pursuit of happiness. We cannot deny them our help on humanitarian grounds any more than we can ignore our own interests.

President Reagan has done a magnificent, masterful job of alerting the people of this country to the need for a strong defense. We cannot afford another namby-pamby leader like President Carter who allowed us to stand still. Look at how technology has transformed your personal life in the past ten years and consider the wondrous advances that must have been made in the science of weaponry—advances that you and I cannot yet know about. We must keep a continual flow of new weapons in the pipeline, like the Red Queen in *Through the Looking Glass,* who had to run as fast as she could just to stay in place.

In today's world we have to consider two types of wars. It is patently imperative that we maintain at least a modicum of balance in the nuclear arms race. It is good to see our leaders making progress on nuclear arms limitation; I only pray that American negotiators are absolutely sure that we have a means of early detection that the Soviets might be abusing any facet of a nuclear arms limitation treaty. For seventy years we have watched the Soviets retreat from their treaties. Moscow is singing a new song these days, and the tune is catchy, but let us make sure that the actions harmonize with the words.

Actually, the next war will be a conventional one. I do not think that either the Russians or the Americans are suicidal enough ever to punch the red button and I believe that the Good Lord would step in to prevent

nuclear war, if need be. But I think that there will always be skirmishes—international power plays—and
we must be ready to respond to them, particularly in
the Americas. Long ago President James Monroe declared that a threat by a foreign power against anyone
in the Americas was a threat to the United States, and
the Monroe Doctrine is still valid.

We cannot allow communist governments to take
over in Central and South America. On the other hand,
we must deal with reality. We have a stupid history of
supporting repressive dictators simply because they
are anticommunist, and there is no more effective rec-
ipe for stirring up communist sentiment among the populace. We must replace that policy with the common-
sense approach that a dictator of the right is no better
than a dictator of the left.

I am a bit of a maverick on this subject, driven to it
by a sense of realism. Those conservatives who lump
me in with themselves will scream in anger when I
suggest that we establish full diplomatic relations with
Cuba.

But why not? We recognize China, the Soviet Union,
and the satellite states of the USSR. They are every bit
as communist as Fidel Castro.

The *great* accomplishment of President Nixon was to
establish relations with the People's Republic of China.
(We will address his great crime in the next chapter.)
The Chinese are now our friends and partners in economic and cultural exchange. Where communism is
entrenched, let us deal with it realistically.

Yet we ostracize Castro, alone among communist
leaders, and as a result we make him more anti-U.S.
than ever. The only way we can wean Castro from the
breast of communism is to feed him the mother's milk
of democracy. Trade with him for sugar and the

world's finest cigars. In return give him the tools to help his people rise from poverty and anguish. If he accepts the bargain he will have no choice but to become less antagonistic toward us and less expansionistic toward the rest of the Americas, and we are then insiders getting an insider's view.

The great tragedy of our military budget is that it is so high. Every American is uncomfortable with the billions we spend on defense, because we are all painfully aware of how much of that is wasted. Cost overruns are rampant, and some of the greatest patriots of recent times have been those Americans who risked their careers to point out abuses. Is there a taxpayer in the country who can understand why this continues? Why cannot a President, any President, appoint a single, capable individual to dig into the morass of the military-industrial purchasing system and clean it out? Show a man a haystack contaminated by huge clumps of horse manure and he will have no trouble cleaning out at least the most obvious, noxious piles—if he is willing to get his hands dirty.

Since, a few paragraphs above, I angered the conservative, let me now give equal time to the liberal. One quick and easy way for us to get more bang for our military buck is rather obvious. When you award a contract on the basis of competitive bidding, why not —quality of workmanship being equal—give it to the lowest bidder? It is difficult for me to understand why we continue to place such enormous and costly constraints upon competitive bidders. Quality and price take a backseat to the proper mix of ethnic workers, male/female, black/white/Hispanic/Asian, able-bodied/disabled. Do you suppose that the Soviets put such constraints upon their military suppliers? Of course not.

Now I hear the liberals screaming: How will the disadvantaged get jobs unless we force business people to hire them?

That one is simple to answer, and there are millions of women, blacks, Hispanics, Asians, and disabled workers out there who can answer it. They will shout out the answer: We will get the jobs by proving that we are harder, better, more competent workers than the average. And we choose to do it this way because it preserves our dignity and builds our pride. It makes us feel more a part of this great American dream.

When will we learn that the way to remove the onus from "second-class" citizens is to stop treating them as second-class citizens?

There are men and women out there of every race and color who still believe that the best defense is a good offense.

20

POWS and
MIAS

O<small>N</small> <small>MY RIGHT WRIST IS A RED BAND, IN-</small>
scribed:

Sgt. Joseph Matijov
Missing in Laos
Feb. 5, 1973

Fifteen years!!!
We have no way of knowing with certainty whether
Sergeant Matijov is alive today. In fact, shortly after
his reconaissance aircraft was shot down over Laos,
government officials informed his parents that he was
dead. Not until *five years later* did his poor grieving
mother learn of excellent eyewitness reports that he
was alive when he parachuted into Laos. His name,
along with those of the other occupants of the aircraft,
was stricken from the list of known live prisoners of
war because he had the misfortune to be captured

eight days *after* the Paris peace accord was signed, and because yellow-bellied U.S. officials did not want to rock the boat. It was not tragedy enough that the Laotians shot him down; so did his very own government.

And he was only one of the more than six hundred American fliers who went down over Laos—and disappeared seemingly forever.

This is statistically curious. We know that 39 percent of the American fliers who bailed out over Vietnam survived. Can we imagine that in Laos no one survived? Of course not. There is irrefutable intelligence evidence of the movements of Caucasians in Laos. A few personal effects have been smuggled out . . . a couple of photos of prisoners in captivity . . . a class ring from the Air Force Academy. We *know* that Americans are being held in captivity in Laos and I *know* in my heart that Sergeant Joseph Matijov lives.

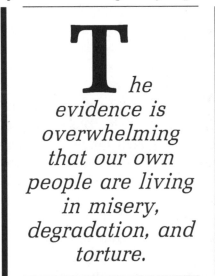

The evidence is overwhelming that our own people are living in misery, degradation, and torture.

The evidence is overwhelming that our own people are living in misery, degradation, and torture.

One Laotian official admitted in 1973 that his government held "tens of tens" of American prisoners. That means hundreds, gang.

According to former Congressman Bill Hendon, now an official of the American Defense Institute, "They're all over the place. Those of us who have seen the intelligence know."

Hendon has hard evidence to back up that statement, such as an eyewitness report dated April 1987 and submitted to American military intelligence experts. It stated that a U.S. military officer named Morgan Jefferson Donahue and five other unidentified Americans were being held in a mountain prison camp in central Laos. The author noted: "This is very urgent because my friends in Laos are afraid that these men will be moved or killed."

A second intelligence report, from a completely unrelated source, said this: "I was a guard at the Boulafa District Prison in the summer of 1987 and I was guarding two American POWs and they are Morgan Jefferson Donahue . . . and H. P. Stevenson." (Stevenson was aboard a gunship shot down in 1972; intelligence reports indicated that nine of the fourteen crewmembers survived.) "One of these men has made two unsuccessful escape attempts and as a result was given an injection of brain-washing drugs. His memory is completely gone."

Despite these and many other reliable reports, Sergeant Joseph Matijov, Morgan Jefferson Donahue, H. P. Stevenson, and their fellow sufferers are as good as dead. They have remained in their special hell for what one of the few good guys in Congress, Congressman Robert Dornan (R–CA), calls "fifteen god-awful years." Or more.

We hear a great deal about a handful of American hostages in Lebanon—and I grieve for them—but we hear nothing about the POWs and MIAs still held prisoner in the concentration camps of Southeast Asia. Our news media have remained curiously uninvolved. I would get down on my hands and knees and kiss the rear end of any major media figure who would focus public attention on the plight of our lost brothers.

Four U.S. Presidents have done nothing for them. The government would like to believe we have forgotten them.

The hell we have! They still live in our hearts and they always will.

How did all this come about?

At the Paris negotiations to end the Vietnam war, Secretary of State Henry Kiss-As . . . excuse me . . . Henry Kissinger . . . had a list of 2,400 names of POWs and MIAs that he was prepared to present to Vietnamese officials. He wanted to demand an accounting. But the treaty had been drawn and was ready for signature, so Kissinger and his aide, later President Reagan's National Security Advisor Robert McFarlane (and, I assume, his boss President Nixon) scuttled the issue so as not to delay the end of the war. Kissinger and McFarlane never presented the list. The American government made the fatal and false assumption that, when the war ended, our POWs would be returned and our MIAs would be accounted for. Only later would they realize the consequences of making a pact with the Devil. (No wonder McFarlane tried to commit suicide after becoming entangled in the Iran-Contra Affair; he *should* be riddled with guilt.)

But why in God's name have we allowed fifteen years to pass without righting this incredible wrong? The unofficial government attitude was enunciated by the late CIA Director William Casey. During a meeting attended by Hendon, Dornan, and two other Congressmen, Casey said, "Of course we left prisoners behind. We fucked up. My job is to make sure we don't fuck up again. What do you want us to do, inflict an instant hostage crisis on President Reagan?"

In a word, *yes!*

But a handful of concerned Congressmen can get no action. Congressman Dornan says of Congressman Steve Solarz (D–NY), chairman of the House Subcommittee on Asian and Pacific Affairs: "I've begged him to bring Kissinger, Bud McFarlane—Nixon himself—before a congressional committee, under oath. Subpoena them if they won't come voluntarily. And tell us exactly what in holy hell happened fifteen years ago to let American heroes rot."

Hendon goes further when he declares: "Henry Kissinger ought to get on a plane tomorrow and go get them. He left them; he ought to bring them home."

I will go even further. In my opinion you can forget Watergate, forget the fiasco of the Iran-Contra Affair, forget who slept with whom—this is the most heinous political crime ever perpetrated upon Americans. The men responsible are Kissinger, McFarlane, and Nixon. Put them in a bamboo cage and let them live in their own defecation for fifteen years!

One who could tell them all about it is Navy Captain Eugene "Red" McDaniels, one of our most decorated fliers, recipient of the Navy Cross, two Silver Stars, several bronze stars (with a "V" for valor), two Purple Hearts, and the Legion of Merit. Red was shot down over North Vietnam in 1967. His parachute hung up in a tree, and when he extricated himself he fell fifty feet to the ground and crushed two vertebrae in his back, leaving him partially paralyzed. When he was captured by North Vietnamese troops he expected medical treatment; instead, he spent three days undergoing the special agony of the "twisting rope" torture, trussed up and hung into the air feet first, with his arms lashed behind his back.

Red was one of the "lucky" ones. He was freed after

six long years of captivity and, since then, has never stopped working to free his brothers. "The Vietnamese believe that through those hundreds of men they have, they can repay this country for all the bombing we did over the years," he explains. "That's the mind-set the Vietnamese have and that's why it's so critical that we get these men out of there."

Think about it. Some of these men—our countrymen —have been hostages for as long as twenty-five years. For them, the war still goes on. They were cannon fodder during the fighting; now they are dung on the jungle floor. This is an outrage second to none in our history. What must they think of America? What must they think of a democracy that has let them rot for a quarter of a century? If and when they are finally freed, could you blame them if they denounced us? I couldn't.

> **A**s *long as* one *American is* held hostage, we are all held hostage.

President Theodore Roosevelt once remarked that one American hostage was one too many; it is too bad that Sergeant Matijov did not serve under him. I just do not see how we can countenance the situation one day longer. How long are we going to continue to let the government kick American boys in the ass?

We need a President like the old Rough Rider, one who speaks softly and carries a big stick—and is not afraid to bash a few heads with it. We need a President who is unafraid to take the necessary steps to free our

brothers, who realizes that as long as *one* American is
held hostage, we are *all* held hostage.

As I write this, President Reagan has only a short
time left in office. He has lived with this problem during his entire presidency, and he has failed to solve it. I
say to him: A lot of us love you, Ronnie, but if you want
to go out as a hero, bring 'em home!

We also need a Congress that will back up a strong
President, and we do not have it. At this very moment
our own government is releasing classified files regard-
ing our POWs and MIAs to the North Vietnamese, but
it refuses to release that same information to the
American public, or even to the families of the unfortunate men. Congressman Robert Smith (R–NH) has in-
troduced legislation to make this information available
to all Americans, but he is meeting resistance in Congress. Why? Because our elected and so-called representative officials refuse to face up to the problem. "It
makes me angry," Smith declares. "We've got five or
ten Congressmen who are really working intently on
this issue. There ought to be 435 Congressmen and a
hundred U.S. Senators working on it, but we don't have
them."

Do not ask your Congressman to support Rep.
Smith's bill. *Tell* them to! *Tell* those gutless fakes of
democracy that either our boys come home or *they* go
home.

There are several ways we can get the necessary job
done. The first step is to pay the countries of Southeast
Asia the $4.7 billion that President Nixon promised
them for the rejuvenation of their economies. Congress
never voted to authorize the money, and so, from the
perspective of the foreign governments, we reneged.
Pay that money now in return for a complete and veri-

fiable accounting of every missing American. Demand proof of those who died and demand the return of those who live. Back it up with a vigorous, on-site inspection.

To those who say that we should never ransom hostages, I say, "Baloney!" What do you think the Iran-Contra Affair was all about? We ransom hostages all the time; we just do not like to admit it. Do you think that hollow principle means anything to Sergeant Matijov?

That effort failing (perhaps due to a reticent Congress), the President should pursue private channels. Congressmen Smith and Dornan are working with Hendon and McDaniels on just such a plan. They put together an organization called Home Free and conducted a national survey, which concluded that 42 percent of the American populace—80 million Americans —is willing to pledge $25 apiece in order to establish a mega-reward for the return of a single American hostage from Southeast Asia. Home Free has launched its fund-raising drive, and when the money is pledged it will spread the word loudly enough so that every prison guard, soldier, bureaucrat, housewife, and garbageman in Southeast Asia hears it: Bring just one American hostage home from Southeast Asia—we don't care how you do it—and we will pay you a reward of *one billion dollars!*

There are far worse ways to spend your money, gang. Send in your pledge *now* for $25 to:

Home Free
The American Defense Institute
P.O. Box 2497
Washington, D.C. 20013

You do not have to send a dime now; just pledge to do so on that happy day when someone claims the reward.

If money does not work, the President should take the case to the World Court in Geneva and ask for a resolution of the problem. This probably would be ineffective, for if communist governments will not respond to money, why should they respond to law? But it would establish a theoretical basis for the action that now must follow.

Finally, after exhausting other means, it is time to wield the big stick.

Mr. President, do you want to see one of the greatest possible examples of American patriotism in action? Just call for a volunteer army to go in and rescue our POWs. They will come from all over the land, young and old, military and civilian, men and women, black, white, Hispanic, Asian, *and* disabled. They will show you that there are still millions in this country who give a damn about other Americans. They will bring with them a military fervor unseen in this country for decades, and I will be among them.

Recruit them. Train them. Arm them.

Then give the communist governments of Southeast Asia twenty-four hours' notice to release our brothers —or face the consequences.

Send our volunteer army off to its war of liberation with these words from President Theodore Roosevelt ringing in their ears:

"A man who is good enough to shed his blood for his country is good enough to be given a square deal afterwards."

21

Freudian Dreams

W<small>E MOVE NOW TO A DISCUSSION OF ONE OF</small> the primary reasons for our social lethargy.

My sister Lorelle, who stood 5'4" and weighed only 106 pounds, could shoot a round of golf in the low 70s —from the men's tees. She was a talented young girl who, like anyone else, had problems. She was obsessed by the fact that there was no mother around to nurture her, and she seldom saw her father. During that upsetting time of the early teens, when she was becoming a full-blown woman, she began to exhibit the classic signs of manic-depression. My father took her to a psychiatrist, who institutionalized her. During her stay in the hospital, the psychiatric team administered more than three hundred electroshock treatments, each one sending her brain into convulsions, burning away her mind. She never had a chance to get better. At the age of fourteen she underwent a deep frontal lobotomy and remained a zombie until her death years later.

Today's psychiatrists probably would not have treated her with electroshock and certainly not with a lobotomy. They might well have prescribed lithium, a true wonder drug for the manic-depressive. The science of psychiatry has progressed; but its art has not.

Here is where I differ with psychiatrists, who, as a group, are among the greatest pabulum-pukers in society today. They would have you believe that their art is an absolute science, and that is a terrible disservice to us all.

This fraud began with Freud, and there is ample proof that he was one of the craziest men ever to walk the face of the earth. Yet there are still countless psychiatric disciples who subscribe rigidly to his theories. Not all are Freudians. There are Jungians, behaviorists, and even Horneys. Each argues vehemently

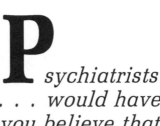

Psychiatrists . . . would have you believe that their art is an absolute science, and that is a terrible disservice to us all.

that his school is the correct one. Perhaps those who best approach the outer edges of reality are the eclectics, who sample a bit of each philosophy and do not know what they really believe.

In sum, psychiatry is a mishmash of theories, and this is a permissible state of affairs until the psychiatrist takes the flying leap from art to science and proclaims himself to be: An Authority.

Flip the dial on your TV or radio, skim through a

newspaper or magazine, and you will find a legion of psychiatrists telling you how to live your life. Sometimes they add disclaimers: *maybe* you should consider this . . . *perhaps* the problem stems from this . . . But even if they hedge, the effective message is that they know how to live life better than you and I. And they seem to have a single prescription for any ailment that plagues society, from hysteria to hemorrhoids. They stroke their usually-bearded chins, gaze into space as though communing with the eternal muse of wisdom, and mumble sagely, "You should get some counseling."

If you believe it, you should have your head examined.

There is one role that psychiatrists serve in modern society that is, regrettably, legitimate. The few good psychiatrists are superb listeners. We all need someone who will listen to us and we have reached an unfortunate state of life where listening is a rare commodity.

Many people never have learned how to listen, and this includes a goodly number of television interviewers who are too busy framing their next question to really listen. The lack of good listeners in our society is a prime cause of our general frustration and apathy. Our politicians certainly do not listen to us. Often we find ourselves surrounded by coworkers, family members, and so-called friends who also refuse to really listen. Confronting societal deafness, we simply stop speaking what is truly on our minds. Ultimately we blow up from the resulting pressure.

So if you need someone who will listen and you can afford to pay an arm and/or a leg per session (that will get you through four 50-minute hours), a psychiatrist can play an important role. It is when he opens his mouth that he causes problems.

The basic message of modern psychiatry boils down to this: You are not responsible for your own problems. They are the fault of your mother, father, siblings, teachers, priests, ministers, and rabbis. They are the fault of society. The upshot is to take away the responsibility from the one person who is most at fault for your problems: you.

We thus have a society ready and eager to believe that its individual and collective problems are caused by others. The next logical progression of thought is: If I am not responsible for my own problems, then I cannot solve them.

So, take the government's welfare handouts. Beat up your wife—it's your father's fault. Rape and murder and shove a stake up the anus of your victim because society has discriminated against you. Shove a needle into your arm—that will serve your mother right.

This is the real craziness of psychiatry. It undermines the age-old truism that the Lord helps those who help themselves.

It took me far too many years to learn this.

It was my best friend Jim Ware, former administrative assistant to California Governor Goodwin Knight, who began the process of teaching both my father and myself that we were responsible for our own lives. "This is no way for a family to exist," he lectured to me and my father on separate occasions. "You two should be together."

To my father, he said, "Your son's a really good guy. He's never asked you for anything. Why do you treat him so badly?"

To me, he said, "Your father's a really good guy. This may be hard for you to understand, but whatever he did to you, he did it out of love."

This *was* difficult to understand. My father had blocked my show business career. He had even con-

spired to throw me into jail! How could I understand—
or forgive—all that?

But Jim persisted, until he finally brought us together
for a reunion. By then my father was gray-haired, aging, and somewhat wary of me. He spoke only briefly
about his attempts to manipulate my life. "I'm sorry,"
he said. "I had to do it."

Oh, I was bitter! I accepted his curt apology, but only
with venom in my voice.

Yet some strange phenomenon began to occur during
this stilted conversation. I saw enough love in the old
man's eyes that I determined to—I was forced to—
keep in touch.

Over the next few years I visited him several times.
The scars were thick and old. He still resented me for
defying his wishes. I still resented him for blocking my
dreams. The wall between us was encrusted with the
residue of ancient grievances.

And yet we both felt a bond we could not deny. I
was his son, and he was my father; we shared half a
genetic heritage.

We had extreme difficulty expressing much of this in
our conversation, which was perhaps why I attempted
right-brain communication. In 1968, as I wrote the
song, "Imaginary Places," I had in mind the image of
my father:

Where do you go
When the doors are all closed,
And no one comes forward to say,
"Welcome home, friend,
Put your journey to end,
Pull up a chair,
Sit and stay."
You go off to imaginary places,

Where a blue sky
Lights a bright and better day . . .

Four more years passed before we were able to enjoy a measure of that fantasy. In 1972 my father, then a
widower, met and married Ann Trainor, who, next to
Kim, I consider to be the most wonderful woman in the
world. She was a Palm Beach beauty many years his
junior and, oh, was she good for him. She brought long-
suppressed laughter to his aging face and a twinkle to
his eye. Most important, she brought us together.

She manufactured patently absurd reasons for me to
visit, and she sat with us, probing our hearts with questions of the past, elbowing her way past our defenses.

I was still bitter—and perhaps always will be. The
closest I could come to an understanding of my father's
actions was to acknowledge that an Irish-American
geezer from the old school of discipline *could* believe
that he was right to intervene so drastically in his son's
life.

Finally, a strange thing happened. I really forgave
him. This was not a conscious decision; it merely occurred. The old wounds no longer mattered.

Then a second strange thing happened. Having for-
given him, I gradually came to realize how I had used
him. I had experienced a life full of so many failures,
and I had consistently blamed them upon one individual: Morton Downey, Sr.

But the old man who sat across from me in Palm
Beach had not lived my life. It was *my life,* not his. I
had committed the classic Freudian sin, blaming *my*
failures upon my father. I could conjure all manner of
outside excuses for the course of my life, but the fact of
the matter was that the buck stopped with Morton
Downey, Jr., not with his father.

And now a third strange thing happened. Slowly, I began to fashion a successful career. I took control of my life as never before.

Dad mellowed, too, finally able to acknowledge and enjoy the success of his son. After so many years of separation and pain, Dad and I gradually became friends. Good friends. And confidants. Ann performed a miracle!

Dad shared his dreams with me, and I shared mine with him. I began to realize with forcefulness that my very own father possessed in his breast the universal urge of all good men and women—that their children will have a better world than they had themselves.

The grand goals I discussed with my father—and I have discussed in these pages—may never be realized in my lifetime. Peace; freedom from poverty, hunger, and homelessness; security; meaningful employment; the harmony of humankind; reverence—indeed, awe—for life; freedom from crime and drugs; joyous health; open communication; and, most of all, universal love, are great, dreamy themes that seem impossible to us. But wouldn't it be nice to think that our children might experience them as my father hoped and prayed that I would.

Whether or not we can realize that cross-generational goal, let us at least show our children that we tried as hard as we damn well could. Civilization began when one person reached out to help another.

How do we change the world?

We start by examining our individual goals. What did you set out to accomplish in life, and how well are you doing? If you are satisfied to sit in front of the television set fat, dumb, and happy, if that was the goal of your existence, then, my friend, your goals were too low.

On the other hand, I do not believe that your goals can ever be too farfetched — only the means by which you try to attain them. Reach for the twinkling stars. Make up your mind to participate truly and fully in this still-great experiment that we call

I do not believe that your goals can ever be too farfetched— only the means by which you try to attain them.

the United States of America.

If the big goals seem unattainable, then break them down into steps. If you do nothing else, find one issue that can become the passion of your life—one issue upon which you and your family agree. Form your own political action group, right there in your own living room. Start as a small cohesive unit centered upon a single idea. Add to that family cluster your friends and neighbors who also agree. You *do* have something worthwhile to say and people *will* listen. They will not all agree with you, but the issue will be out in the open for the majority to decide. That is the American way.

Suddenly you will find that *your* thoughts, ideas, and dreams are beginning to permeate your environment, your town, your county, and your state.

And stop there.

Don't try to change the whole nation. Change your state. This is how America began, as a federation of thirteen sovereign state governments. Today we should have fifty individual nations-unto-themselves, meshed together but retaining far more of their individual identity than is the case. We do not have that situation because we allowed Washington to sell us the giant social melting-pot concept. Well, gang, the people of Massachusetts have a different set of dreams from the people of Arkansas. What concern does a Rhode Islander have about California's prison system? The great illusion that we live under today is that power comes from Washington. As individuals, we feel we have no power; therefore, we do not attempt to exercise any.

The only responsibility of the federal government should be national defense.

The *people* are the state, not the federal government, and it is time the people took back the power that is rightfully theirs. The *only* responsibility of the federal government should be national defense.

We may wind up with thirty states that ban abortion and twenty that allow it. Fine: Live in a state that fits your philosophy.

Just look at the stupid system we have evolved for the collection of taxes. Taxes go from the individual to Washington and then filter *back* to the states. Let the states collect all the revenue, pass a necessary portion onto a greatly diminished Washington bureaucracy, and you will find fewer sticky administrative fingers along the way.

Read the Constitution, gang. You can understand it as well as the great legal scholars who sit on the Supreme Court. It was written by men acting upon a grand dream. They did not cram any ethereal, eclectic, existential bullshit into it.

Our forefathers had one of the grandest dreams ever bestowed upon humanity, a dream that each and every one of us can renew by rededicating ourselves to making this the most humane, the most secure, the most successful nation known to humankind.

We've been there once.

It's time to get back.

This is the message of my latest song, a new music video entitled "We Shall Rise Above It All":

When the night winds blow
And the raging waters grow,
We shall rise above it all.
And in the darkest night
There will be a guiding light.
We shall rise above it all.
Come what may,
We can face what comes our way.
Together we can scale the highest wall.
For our hearts still are strong.
Brothers! Sisters! sing our song
We shall rise above it all.

22

Good-Bye

On my father's eightieth birthday, his friends in Palm Beach threw a fabulous party attended by more than eight hundred people.

Old friends were in attendance, including Douglas Fairbanks, Jr., former Senator George Murphy, and Rose Kennedy.

President Reagan called with his congratulations.

A hired band played. Phyllis Diller cracked jokes. Then came the headliner, the son of the birthday boy.

As I finished singing "I Believe in America," the audience rose, screaming and cheering, their patriotism bubbling over. My dad, sitting in the front row with Kim and Ann, turned to his wife and said, "Ann, where did he learn to sing like that?"

Gentle hands helped him onto the stage. We linked our arms and sang together for the first and last time, belting out his favorite tune, "When Irish Eyes Are Smiling."

I sang once more for him, at his funeral. At the request of his widow and my dear friend Ann, I opened my loud mouth and sang, "Precious Lord."

Thanks, Pop.

I love you.

. . . sorry we wasted so many years.

23
One More Thing . . .

THERE ARE MANY SUBJECTS NOT COVERED IN this book. I, of course, have an opinion on everything, but this was never meant to be a Mort Downey, Jr., encyclopedia, so I chose for discussion those subjects I felt most urgent and relevant to our immediate times. AIDS was mentioned earlier at various points, but it was never my intention to deal with it as a subject alone. God knows AIDS is relevant, *and* urgent, *and* immediate; I didn't want to deal with it anyway. The reasons were personal and private, and I meant to keep them that way. Recent events have changed all that, however.

My brother Tony, my younger brother, a man I have known and loved nearly all my life, has AIDS. And unless there is a miracle, unless the doctors and the researchers come up with a cure for this disease, Tony is going to die.

This is perhaps the toughest subject I have ever had

to deal with. It hurts me and it scares me and it makes me so damned mad, I just want to start kicking ass in every direction. But where *do* you start?

Tony is gay; he officially came out on my TV show, but it is something I have known for many years now. As anybody who has heard me talk for more than five minutes knows, I have always taken a strong position against the so-called "alternate life-style"—homosexuality, bisexuality, perversions of all kinds, whether homo- or heterosexual. The anus is an exit, not an entrance, and as I perceive the sexual practices of these "alternate" groups, anal intercourse is their primary sexual activity. I'm not an expert on AIDS, but I've got to believe that anal intercourse is one of the principal ways of transmitting the disease. It's not just unnatural, it's dangerous, and any person or group of persons who persist in its practice and who defend it are stupid. This is not consensual sex; this is sexual suicide.

And then there are the experts—the doctors and the researchers who keep coming up with theories about AIDS. Some adhere to the theory that a virus called HIV is the culprit. Others say no, that the virus is too weak to be so consistently deadly. Some say that treatment with the drug AZT is currently our best hope. Others say no, that AZT is actually a drug developed to treat cancer and that in the long run it will only further depress the victim's immune system.

The bottom line: nobody knows. And in the meantime doctors in different countries are fighting each other to see who can be first to announce a breakthrough so that the Nobel Prize goes to them. And the drug company of Burroughs, Wellcome is getting rich charging incredible amounts for AZT—literally at prices that make it more valuable than gold. And the taxpayers paid for the research to develop the drug in the first place! Something is very, very wrong here!

In the meantime people keep dying. At first the ratio of AIDS cases was seventy percent gays or bisexuals to thirty percent heterosexual, the great majority of whom were intravenous drug users. Now the figures are fifty/fifty. To date the number of deaths totals almost two thirds the number killed in the Vietnam War. This is not a gay disease; this is a national disaster.

And my brother Tony will probably die, too, but not before I have put up the biggest fight you've ever seen. I am proud as hell of my brother; he is a courageous man and I love him. No, I don't approve of the gay lifestyle he lived, with the drugs and the promiscuity. And no, I will not join the pabulum-pukers who say "Oh, well, to each his own." But I will say that none of us can ignore the cries of help coming from *all* our brothers. We must do all we can to support one another. This is the big one we've all been dreading, and we've got to work together.

I thought I had said good-bye a couple of pages back; now I'll try again. Thanks for letting me share with you. You're great. If ever you wish to share with me, just write me through your TV station. I'll stay in touch, for you truly are my real strength.